PRAISE FOR *MY LIFE IN KENDO*

"Moving through time and space, from a childhood on an early twentieth-century Hawaiian sugar plantation, to life and death adventures in pre- and post-war Japan, then to the Pacific Northwest; the recollections of a brash teen-ager, of a young soldier in the Imperial Japanese war machine, and finally as a highly respected sensei in the art of kendo, Rod Omoto's memoir is rich with historic detail, but especially valuable for his reflections and insights into the philosophy and tradition of the martial arts, which he believed in, and lived, and practiced, till his very last breath. I found his clarity of vision, his honesty and humility, both moving and inspiring."

—Waka (a fellow son of the Hawaiian sugar plantation)

"Omoto Nobuto Sensei was my sensei from the time I started kendo in 1975 and for nearly forty years after that. He played a major part in shaping my childhood, my early adulthood, and beyond. What he taught me is part of who I am today, and his teaching continues well beyond his passing. His leadership was full of encouragement to do better, rather than to scold. I remember him saying, 'Now you've got the mechanics,' which implied there was so much more than the physical aspect. He said a good teacher is just one notch stronger than their student. It was always obvious that his own tough early life and his dedication to hard training were at the core of his teaching."

—Doug Imanishi (Head Instructor, Seattle Kendo Kai)

"Sensei's instruction was focused on bringing out the best in his students. He never said, 'This is no good, that is no good.' Instead, he might say, 'I'll be in trouble if you do something too crazy, but don't be bound by preconceived notions. Just do it freely.' He also emphasized the importance of kendo *kata*, and always began training in Tacoma with *kata* practice. Coming from Japan, I used to feel embarrassed when American swordsmen performed kendo *kata* better than I could. Sensei's approach was to help students master not only the movements of the *kata* but also the principles behind them, using a style that truly 'shows, tells, lets you do it, and praises.' Sensei would often tell me, 'Ogushi Sensei (he always used the honorific "Sensei" even when addressing those below him), Japan's Spartan-style, no-questions-asked teaching method won't work in this country. You have to instruct your students carefully and politely.' These words were born from Sensei's many years of experience, so I tried to follow his example."

—Yasuharu Ogushi (former student of Omoto Sensei)

"I had often heard stories from Jim Dixon Sensei about Omoto Sensei. The stories made him into such a figure of legend in our kendo world that I decided to write to him. To my surprise and delight, he replied quickly and suggested we meet for lunch on October 13, which coincidentally was my twenty-third birthday. Naturally, I accepted. We went to a wonderful small sushi place near his house. Right away I wanted to discuss kendo, but with my girlfriend present, he politely avoided the topic, saying simply that 'Kendo is not talking, it's doing.' It was a good lesson. However, when my girlfriend left to use the restroom, Omoto Sensei suddenly turned serious. He had me hold chopsticks as if they were *shinai*, and we talked kendo. It felt as though he could read my thoughts; it was very profound. At one point, he spoke a line that stayed with me: 'If you think, you die.' It was all so pithy and powerful that it nearly brought me to tears. Omoto Sensei was always one step ahead. He moved so elegantly in the world. It was a day that left a lasting mark on me."

—Aaron Garlick (Head Instructor, Taos Kenyukai)

"I was one of the last children to start kendo with Omoto Sensei during his most active time. The environment was magical for a seven-year-old—the uniform, the equipment, bamboo swords, and all the yelling and screaming! As Sensei got older, my *keiko* with him shifted from kendo *keiko* to meals out, visits to his house, and kendo gatherings. During our visits, he often shared stories about living in Kyoto as a young man, studying Japanese and practicing kendo at Busen with his classmates. Reading about those experiences in this book brought back many memories of our times together. I am lucky to have been able to share kendo with Omoto Sensei and to have him a part of my life. I continue my practice of kendo today as a way to remain connected to him."

—Joji Takada (former student of Omoto Sensei)

"Sword sings through silence,
Sensei's wisdom lingers still —
Echoes guide my path."

—Joe Cuendet (former student of Omoto Sensei)

Purple Breeze Press, LLC
purplebreezepress.com

My Life in Kendo

Library of Congress Cataloguing in Publication Data
Names: Omoto, Rod, author, with Charlotte Omoto
Title: *My Life in Kendo*
Description: First edition. | Purple Breeze Press, 2026

Library of Congress Control Number: 2026900300

ISBN Paperback: 979-8-9918895-8-2

All personal photos are from the author.
Photo of Busen, the historic martial arts school in Kyoto, public domain: https://en.wikipedia.org/wiki/Budo_Senmon_Gakko#/media/File:Butokukai_Kyoto.jpg

Photo of Schichotai Transport Base in Hiroshima after the atomic bomb was dropped in August 1945, photo by US Army / Courtesy of the Hiroshima Peace Memorial Museum.

Calligraphy of *Katsu Jin Ken* "the sword that makes life," courtesy of the artist, Aaron Garlick.

Manuscript edited by Rebecca Williams Mlynarczyk.

Book designed by Streetlight Graphics / streetlightgraphics.com

To my late husband,
Gale Schultz,
who loved Daddy

CONTENTS

INTRODUCTION
Charlotte Kazumi Omoto

My father, Rod Nobuto Omoto, led an eventful life. Born in Hawaii in 1918, to Japanese immigrant parents, he studied the martial art of kendo from the age of fourteen. After graduating from high school in 1938, he traveled to Kyoto to continue his studies, one of the few Americans ever to be accepted at Busen, the most revered martial arts college in Japan. In 1942, during World War II, while still a student at Busen, he was drafted into the Japanese military, narrowly escaping death a number of times. After the War, he remained in Japan, working for the Occupation Forces, a job in which he met my mother, Mutsuko. They soon married and started a family. Finally, after many twists and turns of fate, the family emigrated to the United States, arriving in Tacoma, Washington, in 1960.

After a few years living with his sister's family in Oregon, my parents decided that to have a better future, my father needed to get a college degree. Since his training at Busen did not count in the US, he enrolled as an undergraduate in engineering at Oregon State University, graduating with a bachelor's degree in 1966. Subsequently, he got a job in Tacoma, Washington, at an educational furniture manufacturing company. While living there, my parents were invited to the Tacoma Buddhist Temple, where my father began to teach kendo to the Boy Scout troop that practiced at the temple. From that beginning, he took the opportunity to revive kendo in the Pacific Northwest, teaching in various dojos in the area. He enjoyed going to tournaments in California and British Columbia and earned the rank of Seventh Dan. He was the founding Charter President of the Washington State Kendo Federation, now known as the Pacific Northwest Kendo Federation, and he was one of the founding members of the University of Washington Kendo Club.

During the more than fifty years my father lived in the United States, he didn't share much about his previous life, and he hardly ever talked about his wartime experiences. I have learned that this is not uncommon among those returning from a war. But, feeling the need to share some of these experiences with my sister and me, he enrolled in a writing course at Tacoma Community College, where he began to draft some of the stories that appear in this book. His instructor, Carol Church, encouraged him to write about his many fascinating experiences and suggested an organizing theme for the stories derived from *Go Rin No Sho*, the classic kendo book by Miyamoto Musashi. Although Musashi is a historical person (1584-1645) known for his swordsmanship (he won sixty-two duels and never lost one), he has now become a larger-than-life figure, known to all Japanese. His book is divided into sections entitled "Ground," "Water," "Fire," "Wind," and "Void." My father, who was very familiar with Musashi's book, felt that his life, in some ways, reflected these five elements, with his early life in Hawaii as "Ground," his experiences at Busen in Japan as "Water," his military service during the war as "Fire," followed by his life in Japan after the war as "Wind" and his life after my mother passed away as "Void." Following his wishes, I have used these concepts as chapter titles.

Over several decades, my father's interest in pursuing this writing project waxed and waned. When he passed away in 2013 at the age of ninety-four, numerous versions were scattered on his computer. After his death, I felt the need to consolidate different versions and incorporate orphaned sections into their appropriate chapters. I found that details of certain events and whole periods—for example, his life after coming to the United States—were totally missing. But the choice of contents was my father's, and I decided not to fill in those gaps. I also did not attempt to corroborate his version of events except for consulting my own recollections, talking with my sister and a couple of cousins, and referring to a video interview he recorded decades ago. So, as with anyone's recollection of events in the past, there are bound to be inaccuracies or exaggerations. He might also have put a spin on certain events as a result of an afterthought. However, I tried my best to maintain his voice in the narrative. Indeed, I often heard his voice in my mind as I was compiling this book. I suspect these stories might have been his way to share his history with my sister and me.

The photographs used throughout the book are primarily from our family collection. Many were selected by my father for inclusion, but I have chosen a few others that I found after his passing. And a few, of historic interest, were obtained from internet sources.

I assume that many readers are already familiar with kendo terminology and may also know some Japanese. The first few times a kendo term is used in the text, I include an explanation set off with commas or parentheses. Readers who would like more detailed explanations will find a wealth of information and videos about kendo on the internet. The same is true for Japanese words used in the book. As in any language, many Japanese terms defy simple definition. Thus, I hope readers will take the definition of terms like *zanshin* or *Katsu Jin Ken* with a big chunk of salt. Japanese terms are pronounced with each vowel as a short vowel. For example, sake, the Japanese term for rice wine, is pronounced with a short "a" and a short "e." *Kote*, the term for right forearm hit and also the protective glove in kendo, is pronounced with a short "o" and a short "e."

One of the last decisions I had to make as I put this book together was choosing a title. It was then that I remembered how my father often told his students, "Kendo is my life." It was true for him to the core: in his body, mind, and heart. Although he lived an active, well-rounded life as a husband, father, and friend, kendo was the theme running through his whole life from childhood through advanced age. In the pages that follow, I hope that readers will come to understand what he meant when he said, "Kendo is my life. It has been the path, the *Michi* to the door to eternal life, the *Do*."

1
Ground
地

When I was a boy growing up in the village of Wahiawa in the Territory of Hawaii, I thought I knew all about sword fighting. I had learned to fight by watching chambara movies. These were films featuring heroic samurai, somewhat like cowboy Westerns in the US. My friends and I saw these movies at the Wahiawa Japanese Theater. We used to call it the "tin can" theater because it was made of corrugated galvanized sheets of metal. When it rained, it sounded like several machine guns were being fired at you from the roof, all at the same time. The theater was small, dirty, and smelled like an outhouse. The admission charge for these movies was 15 cents. Sometimes they were free.

We kids used to munch on 5 cents worth of cracked seeds as we sat on wooden folding chairs and watched the chambara movies. The films were silent, but *benshi* (live narrators) imitated the characters' voices and re-created their dialogue. The best orators were great shouters. They could grunt and thud, shout *kiai*, and groan in authentic-sounding death throes as samurai warriors rushed and cleaved and clanged each other in mortal combat. Watching these films, we could see blood gush from severed heads rolling on the ground. Although the films were in black and white, the blood was red to us, and the rusted metal walls of the theater enclosed us in a real battlefield. When the trade winds rattled the walls, it was the roar of battle fires. When it rained, the drops slamming the tin roof became the sound of stamping horses and swords clashing on faraway battlegrounds in Japan, a land I had never seen. But these Japanese samurai were our heroes. Inspired, we would go home and play chambara at the small baseball field or on Mango Street beside the kukui trees and banana patches.

Hoping to make our games look more authentic, my younger brother and I gathered old cardboard boxes, cut them to make samurai armor, and colored them with odds and ends of crayons to look like the *do* (chest protector) and the *tare* (apron to protect the hips and groin) the samurai wore in the movies. We found thick cords in my father's blacksmith shop to tie our armor to our bodies. I also invented the hibiscus sword. After tap tap tapping the branch to loosen and pull off the bark, the remaining white hibiscus branch, smooth and straight, became the sword. I cut a notch by the hilt to become the handle. After we finished our own equipment, my brother and I helped make armor and swords for everyone else.

Soon, our one-street town was protected by cardboard-armored samurai shouting war cries in pidgin, a lyrical conglomeration of Japanese, Korean, Hawaiian, and Filipino, echoing the native tongues spoken in my neighborhood. Just like in the cowboy movies, there were the good guys and the bad guys. I usually played a good guy, so I never got killed. We systematically attacked each other, and when we lost, as in the *Chushingura*, the story of forty-seven Loyal Retainers who avenged their master's death and then committed *seppuku* (ritual suicide), we pretended to kill ourselves by plunging our swords into our stomachs. Luckily, hibiscus is a soft wood. No serious accidents ruined our fun, and our deaths were full of honorable nobility and drama.

Chambara was just kids' play. When my father asked Miura Sensei to teach me kendo, the real training began.

~

On a soft Sunday morning in 1932, when I was fourteen years old, I climbed into Miura Sensei's Model A. We chugged down the rutted clay road of Mango Street to California Avenue, then turned left onto Kamehameha Highway. The speed limit was 45 miles per hour, but that was unrealistic unless we were traveling downhill. I estimated that, if we averaged 30 miles per hour, we would arrive at the Kaimuki Dojo in Honolulu in about an hour. As we crossed the Wahiawa Bridge and the pineapple fields, I was thinking about kendo. I was excited, yes, but also very nervous.

I wanted to feel kendo as a calling, to feel it was my destiny as it was for my movie heroes. But I was going to the dojo in Honolulu, like all obedient Nisei boys (sons of Japanese immigrants), not because it was my wish but instead because my father had decided. I was not consulted. My father and Miura Sensei had discussed my potential and decided that I was to quit football and begin to practice kendo. Had it been thinkable, I probably would have been angry with my father or at least tried to negotiate to participate in both sports. I played end for Leilehua High School, and I was popular and respected for my skill. Football was fun. Now football was *pau* (Hawaiian slang for "finished" or "done"). I wasn't sure that kendo would help my popularity at school. But I *was* sure it would also be fun and exciting.

As Miura Sensei and I passed through the sugarcane fields, I could smell the salt breeze from the Pacific, and I knew we were getting close to Honolulu. My apprehension returned, but I proudly touched my homemade outfit and hibiscus sword for courage, hoping that Miura Sensei would show me how to better play chambara. But he remained silent, saying nothing to me on the trip to the city.

When I entered the dojo, I was so nervous that I'm not sure I remembered to bow, even though I was familiar with the etiquette. But I was impressed when everyone bowed with respect to Miura Sensei, and I was relieved when I learned that I would only be observing that first day. I sat beside Miura Sensei and later watched proudly as he practiced with the lower ranking students as well as other senseis. Playing with other boys in my neighborhood, I thought I was so fierce, but I soon learned that *keiko*, or practice, in the dojo looked nothing like chambara sword fighting. Rather, it seemed to consist of numerous sword cuts and loud cries but with no objectives that I could see.

The combat kendo attracted me more as there were two opponents (other students and the senseis), faster foot movements, which seemed something between a skip and a shuffle, and finally a stomp with a loud shout and a pop to the opponent's head. The kendo helmet was more protective and heavier than my football helmet, and no one was knocked down. It appeared much less dangerous, and certainly more choreographed than football. I was impressed by the complete kendo outfits (*bogu*) worn by the students. My cardboard outfit would have to be replaced by the *keiko-gi* (a shirt made of thick material) and *hakama* (the skirt/culotte part of kendo attire), and for fighting I needed real *men* (protective head gear), *kote* (protective gloves), and *do* (chest protector), not ones made of cardboard.

On the way home, Miura Sensei never corrected, scolded, lectured, or even commented on my hapless bundle of cardboard armor. Perhaps that was his wisdom. Instead, he stopped and bought me an ice cream cone, a treat that would become a ritual later when I had progressed enough to go with him every Sunday to practice at the Kaimuki Dojo in Honolulu. When we arrived home, I was determined to work hard and become a great kendoist so that my father and, especially, Miura Sensei would be proud.

"I'll practice for five hours every day," I exclaimed to impress Miura Sensei, and I meant it. "I'll be the strongest, toughest fighter in Hawaii!"

Miura Sensei chuckled. "That's only part of it, Nobuto," he replied, using my Japanese name. "To the samurai, the sword meant survival. Now kenjutsu, 'the art of the sword,' has evolved to become kendo, 'the way of the sword.'" But I saw little difference. "You don't learn kendo to save 'good' people or kill 'bad' people. The sword is the way to temper and forge your spirit, to make your spirit alive. Today, killing is a misuse, a disgrace, an abuse of the samurai sword. Instead, put everything into *keiko* (practice)," he continued, "cultivating a good attitude."

Then he quoted a favorite line from the great sword saint, Miyamoto Musashi: "A thousand days and ten thousand cuts are needed to acquire comfort and confidence before your spirit is polished and you no longer need to struggle or think about your skill."

I didn't know quite how to respond, but I was sure I would become proficient much faster than he implied. My thoughts quickly returned to my kendo outfit for the remainder of the journey.

The first thing I did upon returning home was to throw away my treasured cardboard *do* and hibiscus sword. I begged my father to buy me the complete kendo *bogu*, just like those of the *sempai*, or advanced students. I couldn't wait to wear the flashy outfit and play like them. But our family was poor, and with seven children, a new outfit didn't come quickly.

Of course, "begged" did not mean the same to a Japanese boy in the Territory of Hawaii as it does to today's American boy. It meant instead that I asked, politely, several times. My father was a frugal man who worked incessantly. He never had time to accompany Miura Sensei and me to Honolulu. Work first to last was his Way, not unusual in our community of immigrants.

~

My father, Omoto Shinichi, was the eldest of five children, four boys and one girl, born to a poor farmer in Kure, in the Hiroshima Prefecture, in 1886. He was a peasant farmer who worked from dawn until dusk in his terraced rice fields. As the eldest son, my father would have inherited the small farm. But whether because of a rebellious spirit, a family feud, individual ambition, or something else, he left Kure in the early 1900s to seek his fortune in the Territory of Hawaii. He had no possessions and no formal education. He probably had not even graduated from elementary school. But he had a peasant's tan and a sturdy, tough body, all 4 feet 10 inches and 135 pounds of him. And he had the ability to work. He had nothing to lose but his pride.

Because my father was the eldest son in the family, he was not accustomed to being told what to do. But things were different in Hawaii. The working conditions were harsh. He was housed with other young men from Korea, China, and the Philippines in a barracks-like building furnished with bedding and a kerosene lantern. Because there was no common language, the workers were awakened by a bell and given orders using body language. He naturally grouped with other Japanese Isseis (first-generation Japanese immigrants), but in such close quarters, they all became friends and created a polyglot language from the various native languages along with Hawaiian words like *hana hana* (work) thrown in. Everyone was paid one gold dollar a day. "One day, *hana hana*, one dollar." My father did not make his fortune in Hawaii. Instead, he worked from dawn to dusk in the pineapple and sugarcane fields and returned to Japan a failure, the second son having taken the place of the first born.

With even fewer opportunities for him in Japan, my father decided to return to Hawaii, to the same hot fields and low pay. Tired of the regimented lifestyle of a field worker, he, like many other immigrants, decided to become independent by learning a trade, mostly at night and on Sundays. Some, like Miura Sensei, chose to become carpenters, some opened grocery stores, but

Shinichi became a blacksmith. He built a workshop next to his house. Working more than a hundred hours a week felt natural to him. Recreation was a luxury he could not afford. His main job was shoeing horses, and his talent for taming and calming frightened animals made him famous within our small community. He also repaired and built the metal-lined wooden bodies of the horse-drawn buggies used in the pineapple and sugarcane fields. As his skills increased, he learned to make the wooden wheels for the buggies by cutting and shaving each spoke, assembling them with a metal strap on the outside, and shrink-fitting them. Later he worked on the springs, axles, and all the other metal parts of the buggies. When automobiles arrived on the island, he quickly learned to fix most of their parts, including two-piece windshields, running boards, axles—everything except the motor. My father was respected in the community as a skilled and meticulous worker.

Once he considered himself successful, he began to think about taking a wife and starting a family. Japanese women did not emigrate to Hawaii like the men, but they did come to marry. One day my father received a letter from Hiroshima with a picture of a pretty young woman, Tameno Oda. She would be his picture bride. So he worked harder, adding a bedroom and a kitchen with a two-burner kerosene stove and an icebox to his workshop house. He wanted to provide comfortable living quarters for his future wife. He did not hire a carpenter like most of the other men. This was not just because he was frugal. He wanted to build his own home with his own hands. When it was completed, it was his personal triumph. He was ready for his bride.

On the day in 1916 when the Japanese men from Wahiawa went to meet their new wives, they jumped on a truck and bumped over the dirt road to the Immigration Office in Honolulu. Nervous and confused, Shinichi stared at the crowd of young women, referring to his picture as he tried to find Tameno. He thought he saw her, a young woman with her head demurely bowed. After he filled out the necessary paperwork, he was introduced to his new wife by an immigration official.

My father and mother.

He had not really considered what to do or say when he met Tameno. His job consisted of providing a house and supporting her and his future family. But, looking at his bride, his heart pounded as long-buried emotions surfaced. He fumbled through his awkwardness as he returned with the other men and their brides to Wahiawa in the now overcrowded truck. During the return trip, the men were no longer jolly and joking with bravado and excitement. The women remained silent unless asked the rare question and, even then, replied shyly with head and eyes averted. The journey seemed like days, but as they arrived in Wahiawa, each man was dropped off at his house to be alone with his new wife. Alone with Tameno, Shinichi's awkwardness increased, and he wished for the diversion of the bumpy ride buffered by the group of male friends.

When he showed her his house, there was no response. Whether she was satisfied or not, she had no choice. Whatever her first emotions were, I can only guess. Mom and I never discussed the emotional terrain she traveled when she met my father and her life and fate in a strange country became sealed.

My first-grade class. I am fourth from the left in the full top row.

The role of wife was formalized in Japanese society, and Shinichi and Tameno produced seven children, in quick succession, five girls and two boys. I was the second child and the eldest son. More rooms were added to the house as the children arrived. And Shinichi took on more work to support his growing family. The children and all household concerns were the responsibility of my mother.

My father was innovative, always experimenting with new ideas. For example, he designed and built a Japanese square bathtub for the family, made from redwood lined with a copper bottom. By word of mouth, these tubs became popular, and soon he was making tubs for all the Japanese families in the neighborhood. He also adapted Model A Fords into cold-storage trucks for use by fish and produce dealers. Our neighborhood on Mango Street continued to grow from the original seven families who lived there when I was a small child, and more people meant more work for my father.

He worked seven days a week, including evenings, using an extension cord to supply light to his workshop. We children all worked with him. I helped by holding the light at night and turning the blower. My brother, Tomio, helped by dragging a horseshoe-sized magnet across the dirt floor to collect nails, bolts, nuts, and washers and then sort them into designated containers. If the nails were bent, we would straighten them. The bolts were oiled and fitted with nuts before we put them into the bins. We worked steadily and precisely and wasted nothing. There was little conversation in the blacksmith shop. Our father spoke to us only to tell us what to do and how to do it.

Our family also raised chickens for eggs and grew vegetables in a garden. My brother and I fished in the Wahiawa River or at Waialua Beach, less a chore than our recreation, but a recreation that was not frivolous but a necessity for the family table. Avocados to spread on bread came from two trees in our back yard. Mangoes, bananas, papayas, and other fruits grew along our street and beside the river, enough to supply everyone in the neighborhood. The only things we bought were rice in hundred-pound sacks and soy sauce. Sometimes meat and imported peaches were purchased for special occasions, but always from someone in our community. We did not shop in stores.

Ours was a spare, frugal, work-oriented life. My father, unlike many other Japanese men, drank only on rare occasions. There were some neighborhood celebrations of traditional Japanese holidays, but food, not drink, was the main focus. The musical entertainment was provided by one of our neighbors, who played the shakuhachi (a traditional Japanese wind instrument somewhat like a Western oboe). Sometimes, my mother attended the Wahiawa Hongwanji Buddhist temple, but not on a regular basis because she was so busy with cooking, taking care of us children, and sewing all our clothes. She even made beer for visiting men. My father was too busy working to attend the temple.

Family portrait. From left, Judy, Sylvia, Father (Shinichi), me, Phyllis, Mother (Tameno), Jean, Ruth, and Brian.

We weren't an unhappy family. But as I grew up, my father, like all Japanese fathers, ruled. He was a man of few words, but when he said something, he meant it. His word was law. When he called my name, I jumped and ran to him answering while I ran. My mother, as a proper Japanese wife, supported him completely and never criticized him. Mother was always kind to us children, telling us stories and teaching us traditional Japanese arts and writing. On Saturdays, my siblings and I attended the Japanese language school at the Hongwanji Buddhist temple.

When I was a child, I never questioned why my mother became a picture bride. Looking back now, it seems unusual since she was from a higher class than my father's family. She had been better educated, graduating from elementary school, and was skilled in reading and writing Japanese. In addition, she had studied the art of flower arranging (*ikebana*) and the tea ceremony (*chanoyu*). But most wonderful to me, and later to all the other kendoists in our community, she was skilled in Japanese sewing.

It was my mother who solved part of my kendo uniform problem. Because of her skill in Japanese sewing, she painstakingly made me a very respectable *hakama* (the skirt/culotte, part of the kendo attire) and *keiko-gi* (a shirt made of thick material for kendo practice). Miura Sensei gave me a wooden *bokken*, or *bokuto* (the practice sword used for practicing *kata*, the ritualized movements in kendo designed to teach proper form, posture, footwork, and timing). I was ready to begin.

But acquiring the kendo *bogu* (equipment) used for sport kendo practice was more difficult. The *men* (protective head gear), *do* (chest protector), *tare* (the thick cloth apron that hangs down to protect the groin and thighs), and *kote* (the gloves worn to protect the wrist) could not be forged or cut from trees. Having the proper *bogu* was necessary, but it was also very expensive. Miura Sensei solved this problem, however, with what today we would call a lease-to-own *bogu*. I could use it for practice and pay for it slowly. He taught me how to make my own bamboo *shinai* (a practice sword made with four long pieces of bamboo held together by leather strips), used to strike the *men* (head), *do* (chest), and *kote* (wrist) of the opponent during sport competition. I was ecstatic. I looked like a warrior and felt confident walking the half mile to practice at the Wahiawa Hongwanji Temple, which was converted to a dojo for kendo during the week. My brother also took lessons, but he was never as passionately involved as I was and soon dropped out.

Miura Sensei, a Third Dan (third-degree black belt), was sensei for the Wahiawa Kendo Club. He provided my inspiration and became my role model. He was my first master and taught me the first rule of the samurai: "Be prepared." Death could come at any time for the samurai of the past, whose enemies were ubiquitous. Being prepared was their only salvation. There are stories of attacks on people in outhouses or while sleeping. Thus, the samurai were constantly alert with their swords close at hand.

I had read stories of the first lessons of martial arts initiation in some dojos. The sensei would tell the novice about the necessity of being constantly alert and then reinforce this rule by striking him fiercely, at any time and often repeatedly. Miura Sensei was kinder. Maybe it would have been better if he *had* struck me because my main problem at the beginning was boredom. I had come to fight, to sword play like I saw in the chambara movies. Instead, he demonstrated how to hold the *boku* and how to draw it in one sweep from the belt and make the cuts. It seemed easy, but lesson after lesson he repeated the same methods, and I was instructed to painstakingly repeat the simple motion of the proper vertical and horizontal cuts.

Miura Sensei was a collector of Japanese swords and a student of the Hoki Ryu school of iaido. Iaido masters synthesized ten *katas* (prescribed sets of movements) from the various schools just as kendo forms were consolidated into the ten *katas*. The iaido forms are generally practiced only by the iaido schools but the *nukitsuke*, *kiri*, *noto* techniques (sometimes compared to fast draw for Western pistol shooters) are part of the curriculum in all kendo schools. These motions are practiced from both standing and sitting positions to allow the swordsman to defend himself in any situation, and, of course, it is practical. It is difficult to win any competition if your sword becomes stuck or if you even have to think about how to draw your sword from the scabbard. Today, extended practice in the three parts of iaido are performed as an exercise in grace and mental composure, another way to temper and refine the spirit.

One day Miura Sensei brought his *habiki* (a metal sword used to practice *kata* that is not as sharp as a true sword), and we took turns practicing the draw, cut, and return. I was nervous at first because I feared I might damage his sword. But sword drawing had almost become routine, and grace meant little to me. I wanted to really test my cut stroke and knew I would prove my skill and be able to advance to more exciting action once I was able to use a real sword.

Finally, Miura Sensei told us he was planning to bring his *shin ken*, a real sword with a razor-sharp blade. This was serious. In fact, the kanji (Chinese characters used in Japanese writing) for *shin ken* means "serious." We were all excited, but Miura Sensei said we had to prepare carefully since we would be using the sword for *tameshi giri* (a traditional way to test both the sword and the kendoist). He told us to think about this, for to use a real samurai sword was a great honor and responsibility. The sword was endowed with almost magical powers. There are legends of how the sword would warn the samurai of dangers and advise him in battle as if it were a living creature. We said nothing when Miura Sensei did not bring the sword to the next practice, or the next. Our anticipation grew.

Finally, one day he brought a sawhorse he had made especially for *tameshi giri*. In feudal times, *tameshi giri* was essential to test the new sword to ascertain whether it was sharp, tough, and flexible enough to return to shape after a particularly strong cut. Today, however, the test is not about the sword but about the cutter, and it has become a discipline in and of itself. In theory, it seems rather simple, but I was to learn differently.

Before Miura Sensei could teach us how to cut, he showed us

how to prepare the materials. The sawhorse must be very sturdy. It is made of 4x4s for strength instead of the typical 2x4s and is 36 to 48 inches long and about 29 inches high. On each side of the lateral portion, nine right-angled L-shaped lag hooks are screwed in about 6 to 8 inches apart. These hooks are used to tie the rice-straw bundles needed for the cutting test securely onto the stand.

The bundle, called the *maki wara*, is composed of a bamboo center (about one inch in diameter) surrounded by rice straw. To make the bundles, we laid the straw on the floor, put the green bamboo at the edge of the straw, and rolled it up tightly. Then we secured the straw with a rope of rice straw and tied the bundle about every eight inches. We usually made about six to eight bundles. After cleaning the basin by the entrance to the dojo, which we normally used to wash our feet before we entered the hall, we refilled the basin with clean water. Then we placed the bundles into the basin to soak overnight.

The next day before kendo practice, we covered the dojo floor with canvas to keep the dripping water from the bundles from staining the floor and to collect the scattered pieces of straw after the test cutting was completed. We next stacked two of the soaked straw bundles on top of each other and tied them securely to the stand horizontally. The bundles simulated parts of the enemy's body—the thigh or the torso. The straw represented the flesh; the bamboo, the bone; and the water, the blood. I imagined the drippings as red blood and the chambara body parts in the awesome carnage of battle.

Despite all the meticulous preparations and ritualized preparations, test cutting appealed to my sense of samurai ferocity. Miura Sensei then demonstrated the cut for us. He stood in front of the stand with his legs spread about two feet apart, pulled out the sword, held it with both hands, and raised it in *jodan* position (high above his head). We stood breathless, moving our eyes to

Miura Sensei, then to the sword, then to the bundles. He took a long breath and slowly brought the sword down until it just touched the bundles. Then with another deep breath, as though he was meditating, he raised the sword and, in a flash, brought it down again, so rapidly it was a blur. We didn't see the actual movement. The sword stopped at the end of the second bundle. Miura Sensei sighed and slid the sword toward him and out of the bundle. With one movement, swinging rapidly but seemingly without effort, he had cut cleanly through both bundles.

Watching my teacher, I remembered my chambara play with the neighborhood boys, where we never did anything slowly or quietly. I thought cutting would be easy. Miura Sensei made it look easy. When it was my turn to try, I was afraid I might cut through both bundles and not be able to stop, slicing into the dojo floor.

I knew I was young, strong, and bigger than Miura Sensei. I gripped the sword firmly in the manner I had been taught, meditated, took a deep breath, and then brought it down with all the force I could muster. I listened for the clean crack, but to my horror, I didn't even reach the bamboo in the first bundle. I was embarrassed and humiliated until my classmates proved to be equally incapable. Some didn't even cut into the first bundle, the sword mysteriously turning sideways. In fact, the best senior student managed to barely cut through the first bundle, never touching the second.

Miura Sensei explained the true technique of the *hasuji* (correct cutting angle of the blade) and the *te-no-uchi* (the correct way of gripping and manipulating of the sword): "If the cutting angle is not in a true line, it will not cut. If you merely use your forearms, or even your whole arm, no matter your strength, it will not cut. Firewood is chopped, splitting because of the grain of the wood. But you are not chopping firewood. You must use your whole body and your *hara* (the center of gravity, located about two inches below the navel)."

We tried again, doing somewhat better. But when he told us to try the *kote* (the wrist as target) and *men* (the head as target) strikes, none of us could cut. This was the most dynamic lesson we had learned illustrating the key importance of *hara*, which Miura Sensei constantly emphasized. The *hara* is the center of gravity of the body and the focal point of balance. More importantly, *hara* corresponds to the spiritual center, the source of *ki*, or life force. When the cut is made, the tightening and thrust of the *hara* provides the power. "The sword is your soul, your spirit, your strength," said Miura Sensei softly. "You and the sword must be as One, *itchi*. The master swordsman understands *ki ken tai no it'chi*, "The Spirit, Sword, and Body are One." It is not your weight or your muscles or your will that cuts the bundle. It is your spirit; the sword is an extension of that spirit. A spirit that is not composed cannot cut. But don't worry," he concluded, "years are required to cultivate your attitude and refine your spirit."

~

I knew I had just begun. After *tameshi giri*, I knew the value of *suburi*, or repetition of basic strokes. I set up a rubber tire from my father's shop for a target and vowed to make at least a hundred cuts daily. "Perhaps fifty would be a more realistic number," Miura Sensei counseled. And he was right. I tried to practice at least fifty strokes per day, but often not even fifty strokes were possible. But I was learning patience and knew kendo was not going to be a quick dash to the goal post. I was no longer bored and paid attention to everything, no matter how trivial it seemed.

Humbled, I now was thankful for the reminder of *rei* (proper etiquette). We bowed to the dojo, the training hall, when we entered and when we exited; we bowed to each other and to the sensei; we bowed at the beginning and end of each *keiko* (practice) with a different partner. We bowed to the *kamiza*, a kind of shrine or altar, located in the front of the dojo. Our *kamiza* was flanked with the flags of Japan and the Territory of Hawaii, flowers traditionally arranged by the ladies of the temple according to the formal school of *ikebana*, and a Buddhist icon. All honored the spirit of the school, connecting the students to a tradition of respect greater than any individual. Miura Sensei reiterated constantly that the sword of the old samurai tradition was to take life, or *satsu jin ken*, but the sword of the modern kendoist is to make life, or *Katsu Jin Ken*. "Just as electrical current can electrocute a person, so also does it make the wheels of industry hum. Just as a razor-sharp knife in the hands of a madman can take a life, in the hands of a surgeon, the same knife can save a life." He wanted to be sure I understood the meaning behind all of these rules. "Kendo is not just stick fighting, Nobuto. The dojo is where you train for your life."

He often told us that he hoped we would never have to use a sword to save our lives as did the samurai during the feudal period of Japan. I was finally ready to hear what he had said at the very beginning of my training: "The training will forge and temper your spirit and give you life by disciplining your spirit. That is the goal of the modern samurai."

Inspired by these spiritual moments, I felt both awe and respect, especially after my pride had been challenged. Yet sport often took precedence over spirit. I was excited, and I wanted to win. I needed to win. I no longer merely endured practice, I embraced it. Indeed, the tradition of kendo is the tradition of practice, not of theory. Confusion is erased by doing. The beginner is initiated into the Way, *rei* by *rei*, *kiri* by *kiri*, until it no longer requires conscious thinking. The martial spirit is exuberant, beginning with a spring to action and a shout. But to win, the sprit and the mind must be calm.

Winning was important to me, and my competitive spirit was strong. I enjoyed tournaments and awards and usually prevailed over opponents in Wahiawa. Finally, Miura Sensei decided I was ready for more serious competition in sports kendo, and he started to take me with him to the Kaimuki Dojo in Honolulu every Sunday for practice.

In Kaimuki then, as it still is today, practice was not segregated by age or rank. When I entered the dojo as a teenager without a rank, I was accepted as part of the group by everyone including Wada Sensei (Fifth Dan), Mikami Sensei and Sugi Sensei (both Fourth Dan) and Miura Sensei (Third Dan). I was expected to observe the same etiquette. No one patronized me or made excuses for me because I was just a kid. I was a participant in kendo, practicing alongside them and with them and accorded respect as a student of the Way. I found my models and my heroes and became a man by becoming a kendoist.

Best of all, I had the whole day with Miura Sensei. He spoke on the drive to and from Honolulu, guiding the discussions and philosophizing about kendo in general, especially the kendo attitude. He rarely talked of techniques. He was a carpenter by trade, and like the great master of the Edo period, Miyamoto Musashi, he related kendo to carpentry. "The swing of the hammer must be straight, Nobuto," he would tell me. "The carpenter must use his energy economically, sure and steady, or he will become exhausted and hit his finger instead of the nail. The muscles are of less importance than concentration. Intent comes from the center of your being, the *hara*. With the hammer and the sword, the swing is straight, and the force comes when you tighten the *hara*. You see how kendo is part of everything I do."

His conversations were also interspersed with questions about my progress in school and comments about weddings and funerals in Wahiawa and sometimes about my family. "Your mother understands more than she realizes about kendo," he commented. Then he chuckled as he added, "More than you know about it, yet." I was incredulous when he said this but did not dare question or contradict him. "Just look at her flower arrangements, her sewing, or her quiet performance of the tea ceremony. She performs the tea ceremony as if it is the last thing she will do in this life. Extending hospitality to another person is a particular occasion never to recur in one's lifetime, so she attempts to make the occasion perfect. Notice her tranquility and stillness in the midst of all you children. Then you'll see."

This was his explanation, but I didn't see, especially since Miura Sensei had neither a wife nor children. Nonetheless, I'd nod agreement, long ago having stopped doubting him. After this comment, I *did* pay more attention to my mother, admiring her calm attention to every detail in our household. Perhaps, she, too, was a master, I thought, after Miura Sensei told me the story of a tea ceremony master who was challenged by a samurai to a sword duel. The tea master consulted another samurai to help him in this predicament. The samurai told him that he was not a sword fighter, but a great master of the tea ceremony. "Therefore, you cannot challenge this samurai with sword technique. Use what you know best to meet the challenge. Draw your sword, face your opponent directly, slowly close your eyes, pull your sword high above your head with both hands, and act as though your opponent is the guest of honor in your tea ceremony. Wait until you feel something cold come down on you. That's when you bring down your sword." The tea master did exactly as he was told and waited for a long time, but nothing cold came down on him. Slowly, he opened his eyes. To his surprise, he saw the challenging samurai squatting down with his sword in front of him, bowing and apologizing for his rude behavior in the past.

When Miura Sensei talked to me, there was never a sense

that he was lecturing, and I did not take notes. He was never critical, and I never felt embarrassed. "Concentration is necessary," he might say, but he would never mention that at the previous practice I had been distracted and had wavered as I cut, my *shinai* twisting so that I missed my target by at least six inches. He would question me at times, especially when I felt discouraged. "What are you doing kendo for? For the sport, or for your father, or . . . ?" He would leave his question open-ended and never pressed for an answer. This was for me to contemplate. Then he changed the subject to the one subject I anticipated most eagerly.

"What kind of ice cream will you have today?" he'd ask. "Vanilla," I would always answer. This was the ritual treat for our trip, a great incentive and reward, reinforcing my sometimes flagging enthusiasm for strenuous and usually humbling practice in the dojo. My zeal for ice cream was constant and spurred me to continue.

At home, nothing changed in my life despite my decision to join The Way of kendo. I still worked with my father in the blacksmith shop although his ambition for my kendo allowed him to excuse me if he noticed I was tired from practice. I still liked chambara movies, but I now knew they had no relationship to true kendo. I also occasionally played football with my friends. But I had long ago given up being on the team. Football is a physical diversion, a sport with rules, but a history measured in decades, not centuries. There were no spiritual traditions that I could see in football and certainly not the generational mix I became accustomed to in kendo. In football, the coach was often the only adult involved, except for parents cheering on the sidelines.

To put it simply, I saw kendo as a Way, though vaguely so, and football as a sport. In fact, football was more like the one-hour action segments of the chambara movies, but it was decidedly

American. Kendo is also a sport—and is more and more emphasized as sport—but a sport that does not pass with age. Kendo would change my life and become my life. *Katsu Jin Ken*, using the sword not to kill but to bring life, has become the theme of my practice. It has been refined, but not completed, even now near the end of my life.

2
Water
水

I GRADUATED FROM LEILEHUA HIGH SCHOOL in my hometown of Wahiawa in 1938.

By the time of my high school graduation, I had achieved the rank of Second Dan in kendo, which was a considerable achievement for someone my age. But by then I knew there was so much more to learn. The discipline of kendo required physically demanding practice sessions, but I had finally realized, as Miura Sensei had told me from the beginning, that the real discipline was of myself, to temper and refine my spirit. Although I had won tournaments in Oahu and had once, in 1934, traveled to Hilo on the Big Island with Miura Sensei to participate in a tournament, I felt that my skills were strong, but my character was far from the ideal of the *bushi*, the feudal samurai warrior of Japan.

Bushido, the Way of the Warrior, stresses kindness and benevolence as well as courage. I trained hard yet wondered how far I had really progressed. Was I benevolent or courageous? I didn't think so. My mind was definitely not quiet, and my pride and ego punctured any thoughts of humility. I certainly never considered death as a serious threat, and the concept of *bushido* as "the resolute acceptance of death" was not something I could relate to. No one wants to die, and when Miura Sensei told me that the Way of the Warrior is death, it seemed an arcane thought relevant to feudal Japan but of little consequence in the fragrant Hawaiian countryside alive with the aloha spirit of hospitality and sharing. Of course, I did not openly discuss or question these statements. I trusted Miura Sensei when he said that if I applied myself, someday I, too, would understand. Mostly, however, I was a happy-go-lucky Hawaiian teenager and thought I knew everything I needed to know. To understand the way of the warrior and concepts of *bushido* was not my primary goal.

Inside cover of my 1938 high school yearbook. The phrase after my name in the book is "Common sense is not a common thing."

When I was with Miura Sensei, however, I was ashamed to realize that I was interested in my own welfare and having fun, unlike the samurai warriors of old. In fact, I questioned whether I truly had the right desire and drive to learn kendo beyond my current skill. I was satisfied with where I was, second in rank to Miura Sensei. Swinging a sword to "create my life" seemed crazy since I was quite satisfied with my life as it was—with one exception. I had never been to dances with girls in high school. "Holding a lady is not good," my father said. "Concentrate on kendo." And that is what I did.

Fishing trip with my friends. From right, Walter, Kiyomi, Kaju. I am in front with Kiyomi's younger brother.

I had no girlfriend or social life and didn't attend parties, but I enjoyed what was probably a typical teenager's life in Hawaii at that time. I pole vaulted beside the garage, and my best friend, Walter, and I made fishing poles to catch catfish and bass while wandering along the banks of the Wahiawa River. Along with my brother and several other young men, I traveled to Ka'ena Point, the desolate northern tip of Oahu that still has only a rough dirt road. We would set up camp in the rock caves, build a fire, and fish for ulua all night long. These fish were fierce fighters, and landing one was like winning a battle, though with no threat of death to the fisherman.

My world was small, but I was happy. I had friends and was satisfied by my travels. After all, I went with Miura Sensei once a week to what seemed like the huge city of Honolulu, and my journey to Hilo on the Big Island to participate in a kendo tournament was further than most of my friends in Wahiawa had ever gone.

Budo Taikai, martial arts tournament, at the Hilo Young Buddhist Association.

My father and Miura Sensei had bigger plans for me. They decided I should go to Japan, attend a famous dojo, study with a famous sensei, become a professional kendoist, and then return to Hawaii and teach others. "You should study the true kendo from the world's top sensei, Ogawa Kinnosuke," Miura Sensei told me. "Know it in your *hara*. Chew, digest, absorb all you can learn from Ogawa Sensei, and when you return, adapt it to the Hawaiian way. You cannot directly import Japanese kendo to Hawaii, but you must never compromise the spirit of kendo." My fate was sealed.

There was no discussion about the decision that I should go to Japan just as there had been no discussion when they decided that football was *pau* for me. This was the "way" of the Japanese father. It was just that simple. I would leave in September 1938 just after my twentieth birthday and return to Hawaii a few years later. I could endure almost anything for a short time, I thought. I could understand the language since I had learned Japanese from my mother and at the Japanese language school at the Hongwanji Buddhist Temple. Miura Sensei implied I would have no trouble adapting to life in Japan: "Play dumb and learn everything, good or bad."

I was already a Second Dan kendoist, and everyone expected that I would quickly rise in rank in Japan to return as a young sensei. Teaching kendo would enable me to support a family with significantly less effort than being a blacksmith or a laborer in the pineapple fields. It would also bring honor to my family, especially my father. Ever since the eighth century, kendo has been synonymous with the samurai class and nobility. If peasant boys in Japan played at stick fighting, as I had played chambara, they still could not become professional kendoists. My father's move to Hawaii stirred a bigger aspiration. In a new country, very different from the class-conscious Japan, he could nurture hopes of becoming more than a peasant and bringing honor and respect to his family name. He always identified with Japan, and his *Yamato-damashii* (Japanese spirit) grew in this distant land. A man who constantly worked for his family, his reward would be my success in becoming a Japanese-trained professional kendo sensei.

That summer I continued working in my father's shop and practicing kendo. I almost envied my brother, Tomio, who had developed his interest in electronics after quitting kendo. He patiently gathered parts, studied late at night, and made his own ham radio. I, too, was fascinated by radios, and when Tomio joined the ham radio club and began communicating with people around the world, I wished I could do that, too. I thought that talking to people around the world on a ham radio and taking occasional trips to Honolulu and the other islands were all I would need to have a happy life.

But perhaps the path my father and Miura Sensei chose was more appropriate for me. I was more active and mischievous as a boy than my quieter brother. With my hot temper and stubbornness, traits much less apparent in my gentler, more contemplative brother, the martial arts suited me better. I would train relentlessly, more than any other student, if necessary, to overcome any shortcomings in either my technique or my nature. To disappoint my father was unthinkable.

No one discussed what I might face when I went to Japan. No one thought that culture shock would be an issue. After all, I was Japanese. I had learned the Japanese language from my mother and at the Buddhist temple. My only preparation was to consult a map of Japan to determine the location of Kyoto. All I knew was that I would take a steamship to Yokohama and then a train to Kyoto to the Dai Nippon Butoku Kai Budo Senmon Gak'ko, commonly called Busen.

To prepare for entering Busen, I got my three *shinais* into perfect condition. I also checked my kendo *bogu* carefully and even ironed my *hakama* for the very first time. My *bogu* and *keiko-gi* were still among my major concerns. I had mixed feelings about learning more kendo, and I was quite sure there would be no ice cream in Japan. Moments of philosophy and stories with Miura Sensei, which seemed so serious and inspiring for me at the time (even though I didn't fully understand them), were forgotten. I was still a happy-go-lucky Hawaiian kid. But I would go; there was no choice. And I would bring honor to my family, and especially to Miura Sensei, by succeeding.

Photo taken for my send-off to Japan in 1938.

I remember my send-off. There was a big party with good food. It was a party of enough importance that my mother offered the beer she made and stored under the house to several of the older men, including Miura Sensei. My father never drank, not even for this party, which was as much congratulatory for him as for me. All our neighbors and classmates attended. Everyone in the Japanese community was proud. They felt my success would also be their success. I was embarrassed that I was not as excited about my trip to Japan as my neighbors and friends seemed to be. But I showed humble enthusiasm for my good fortune and genuine appreciation for my father and Miura Sensei for making this possible.

My teacher gave me one of his own books in Japanese as a going away gift. My father had purchased my ticket and would provide the money for my expenses at Busen. It was more than any of the other neighbors in our poor community could have provided. I thanked everyone, especially Miura Sensei. I would treasure the book he gave me even though I was not much of a reader.

Miura Sensei helped me pack. He was pleased with the condition of my *shinais* and my *hakama* and made sure I didn't forget to pack the book he had given me: *Kendo* by Takano Sasaburo Sensei, which I still have and sometimes reread even today. He told me I could read it during my twenty-day journey. "The book will provide a review," he explained, "of the kendo principles we've spoken of. It will also help you practice Japanese. Now you can read the words of Miyamoto Musashi. You will arrive well prepared. And on deck, don't forget to practice *suburi* (kendo exercise in which a sword is swung up and down). Remember, you can do s*uburi* anywhere. You can do it sitting down if there is no room to stand or too much rolling on the ship to gain good footing." I promised him I would study and practice.

I was somewhat interested in *The Book of Five Rings*, which was contained in Sasaburo Sensei's book. Miyamoto Musashi, the author of *The Book of Five Rings*, had become a hero to me as he was to almost all Japanese. Born in 1584, he was the greatest swordsman in Japanese history. I thought I would probably enjoy his accounts of battles, especially since he killed a man in a one-on-one battle when he was just thirteen years old. His book was a short section within the larger book of *Kendo,* and I thought I could read it quickly. I felt I was fluent in Japanese, so I did not intend to study too diligently; *suburi* was more attractive to me than any philosophical discussions. I would keep in shape and be ready for my first practice at Busen. Practice was the practical course of action.

While I was waiting to steam out of the harbor, I started to read the book Miura Sensei had given me. I was surprised to find how difficult it was to translate and understand the book. But I rationalized that this was old-style Japanese. I should be fine with modern Japanese once I reached Kyoto. I assumed Old Japanese was of little relevance to my education.

Unfortunately, I was mistaken about everything I had assumed. I managed to read only the introduction and first chapter, "*Chi No Maki,*" or "The Book of Ground," of *The Book of Five Rings.* It was about twelve pages long and described no action-filled battles. I never read another page after the ship steamed from the harbor, and I never did a minute of *suburi.* What do I remember of the twenty-day voyage? Nothing!

Well, not exactly nothing. I remember the head, the ship's toilet in the hall by my room. My head in the head! I decided I should have learned surfing instead of kendo for this trip because I was seasick the entire time. There isn't anything more miserable. I stood on deck and tried to gulp cool air. I tried to walk. I tried to meditate. I tried to hold my breath, to keep my eyes closed, to keep my eyes focused on one object. I tried eating and not eating. Nothing helped. Lying on my bunk with no movement and no food in my stomach was the best I could do. No reading, no *suburi*—nothing. This was not samurai spirit. Twenty days seemed an eternity. I couldn't wait to set foot on solid ground!

~

There was only one good thing about being seasick during the whole trip. It kept me from worrying about what I would face when I arrived at Busen. Like all young men who practice kendo, I knew the history of this famous school. It was a professional martial arts academy with four departments: kendo, judo, naginata, and kyudo.

Busen, the historic martial arts school in Kyoto, completed in 1899.

The history of Busen was written by kendoists, and indeed, kendo seemed favored in the school. The first head of Busen was Naito Takaharu Sensei (1862-1929), a kendoist. Busen's history began with a concise telegram to Naito Sensei: "*Michi no tame ni kitare!*" ("Come for the sake of The Way"). Leaving his very successful business and dojo in Tokyo, he answered the call.

On October 1, 1905, Bujutsu Kyoin Yoseijo, the first name for Busen, was started with Naito Sensei as the head master. In July 1912, the name was changed to Budo Senmon Gak'ko, and in March 1914, the first class of eight students graduated.

In January 1948, the thirty-fifth and last class graduated fifteen students. During the school's forty-two-year history, students from the northernmost island of Hokkaido to the southernmost island of Kyushu, usually the best kendoists from high schools all over Japan, often from wealthy families, attended Busen. The school was well regarded, perhaps comparable in prestige to the military academies of West Point and Annapolis in the United States, though it was not a governmental institution nor nearly as large as the American military schools.

I don't know how my father and Miura Sensei approached Ogawa Sensei to gain my acceptance to Busen. It was extremely rare for a young man from outside Japan to be accepted. I was one of only two who entered Busen from a foreign country in the whole history of the school. Odate Isao, the second student from Hawaii, studied judo and graduated in the twenty-seventh class in March of 1941. Only two graduates of Busen later became permanent residents of the United States, Mikio Hattanda of Santa Barbara, California, and myself. I would have graduated in the thirty-first class in 1944, but I was drafted into the Japanese military in 1942. But that is another story.

~

For now, I will return to the autumn of 1938, when I finally arrived in Kyoto. I don't know what kind of arrangements were made in advance by Miura Sensei or my father, but after I got to Kyoto, I was allowed to live in the dressing room of Kodokan, a dojo that was adjacent to the home of Ogawa Kinnosuke Sensei, the head of the kendo department at Busen. I had various jobs around Busen and in Ogawa Sensei's household—fixing the kendo gear for the young students, taking Sensei's dog, Jiro, for "walks" on my bicycle, and helping to clean Kodokan and Sensei's house. In addition to providing my housing, Ogawa Sensei taught me a lot about the traditional Japanese culture of

Kyoto, how to endure and adapt to cold and suffering, and how to gain confidence and become a Nihon kendoist.

Unfortunately, I was not able to begin my studies at Busen immediately. My poor preparation in Japanese proved to be a major hindrance. Thus, Ogawa Sensei arranged for me to attend Seiho Chugak'ko (high school) for two years. Upon graduation from the high school, I took the entrance exam for Busen and promptly flunked despite my two-year immersion in a Japanese school system. Then Ogawa Sensei arranged for me to attend classes in classic Japanese and Chinese language in the evenings in Ritsumeikan Daigaku (a university in Kyoto) to help me pass the entrance exam.

~

I had learned the basics of kendo, the "Ground," in Hawaii, but when I arrived in Japan, the ground shook, and I had to adapt. *Jishin* is Japanese for "earthquake." Another Japanese term with the same pronunciation can mean confidence. "*Ji*" is "self" and "*shin*" is trust, so perhaps it means that when one trusts oneself, it produces confidence that can be as profound as an earthquake.

Once I finally passed the entrance exam and enrolled in Busen, I had no time to analyze or be nervous. I did what others told me and thereby adjusted to the circumstances ("*rin ki o hen*") of my new life. Day in and day out I followed this routine:

Ne te oki te;
tabe te ugoi te ne te oki te.

寝て　起きて
食べて　動いて　寝て　起きて

Translated into English, this means:

Sleep, then get up;
eat, then move; sleep again; then get up again.

Eating meals at the noodle shop was the only time—practically no time—I had for thinking as my body just got on with the job of eating by itself. "Move" meant doing my chores, which continued because I remained in my room at Kodokan, never living with my fellow students, even after I graduated from Japanese high school, completed night school classes, and was formally accepted as a student at Busen. Of course, "move" mostly meant kendo practice.

Every morning from 6 am to 7 am, I would do *asageiko*, morning practice, at Busen. For the first year, we only trained *kirikaeshi*, the basic exercise of repeating side head cuts. That was for the whole year! This is a very basic cut, and other students who had been tops in their high schools were bored and would complain that they had already trained *kote* (wrist cuts) and other cuts considered more advanced. When they complained, "All you do is *kirikaeshi*, the *sempais* (senior students) would answer, "If you don't like it, go home!" These were the instructions of Ogawa Sensei, and they were not to be contradicted.

After the morning practice, from 7 to 8 am, we ate breakfast.

From 8 am to noon, I attended lectures consisting of more Japanese language, both modern and classic, and Japanese calligraphy. Calligraphy has long been associated with the samurai. On the first page of "The Book of Ground," Miyamoto Musashi noted, "the warrior's is the two-fold Way of brush and sword, and he should have a taste for both Ways." Young men of the Japanese nobility of the Edo period were educated solely in the Chinese classics and practicing calligraphy. Brush and sword were to be *bunbu itchi* (in accord).

Lunch was from noon to 1 pm. And then more *keiko* from 1 to 3 pm. From 3 to 4 pm was afternoon practice, *koshuka* (short training after regular training). This was the "voluntary practice," which I had already learned was not really voluntary. If you didn't attend, unless you were a senior with other commitments to assist in *keiko* somewhere else, you didn't belong in Busen. After 4 pm, I would go home to study. But I still needed to clean the dojo and do all the chores I had done since arriving in Kyoto.

Finally, it was time for evening practice at Kodokan, when I would practice with Ogawa Sensei. Kendo practice was a minimum of about six hours per day, but still less than the *keiko* that Miyamoto Musashi had done during his lifetime! You could never practice too much.

After evening practice, as before, I fixed *dogu* (kendo gear) and made *shinai* (bamboo swords), scrubbed the baths of Ogawa Sensei or Waka Sensei (Ogawa's son-in-law), walked the dog, and closed the gates. Exhausting, grueling, yes, but it all became habit, "no big deal." I was not conscious of how I was absorbing all these activities, known not in my mind but in my body, heart, and spirit, transforming me into a kendoist. I simply recalled what was said to me by Wada Kyoichiro, my *sempai*: "Everything you do, Nobuto, is kendo practice. It is your responsibility to observe and learn. Practice, practice, practice!" I was not explicitly forced to do anything, and I was complimented so rarely that I can recall no direct encouragement. But my spirit was on fire. I felt no pain and practiced and practiced and practiced.

Kendo, I thought, is about adapting, adjusting, being ready for any situation, for any emergency. Miyamoto Musashi declares in "The Book of Water" of *The Book of Five Rings* that the "spirit of the *Ni Ten Ichi* school of strategy is based on water." The first book, "The Book of Ground" is the body of The Way of strategy, as "a straight road mapped out on the ground." but with "water as the basis, the spirit becomes like water. Water adopts the shape of its receptacle; it is sometimes a trickle and sometimes a wild sea. Water has a clear blue color." The principle of strategy is to know one thing and thereby the "ten thousand things"—things written in "The Book of Water."

"Adapting, yes," Ogawa Sensei mused as I hesitantly mumbled what I thought was a profound insight, hard earned because I now knew classical Japanese. I had been privately studying *The Book of Five Rings*. "But in the *Mizu No Maki*," he continued, "Musashi is discussing application, or adapting, the techniques of swordsmanship." He paused, then slowly explained, "*Bushido* (The Way of the Warrior) is not something you adapt to your life. Instead, it means changing your life in almost every way. You began with Miura Sensei, but the sword will continue to change you as long as you practice. You will never be finished. More is expected of the *bugeisha* (someone trained in the martial arts as practiced by the samurai) than of an ordinary person. Reflect on that."

I reread the "*Chi No Maki*" ("The Book of Ground") and focused on Musashi's words that "the true value of kendo cannot be seen within the confines of kendo techniques." Yes, I had learned the basics of kendo in Hawaii, the ground of kendo: the *Chi*. I had learned how to breathe differently, into the *hara*. Balance and stability come from the *hara*. I had watched animals; their bellies, not the upper chest, expand and contract with the breath. The power does not come from the head or shoulders. "Uptight" is slang in the United States for tension, and indeed, the shoulders are raised, the breath shallow, and the chest heaves when a person is uptight. The breath of a baby is seen as the stomach area (the *hara* area) rises and falls. Such is natural breathing. And swordsmanship is based on what is natural. The kendo stance, solidly rooted to the ground, is powerful. The sword cuts, not from shoulder action, but from the natural pull of gravity, guided to its target by the right hand, and cinched from the *hara*. I recalled the *tameshi giri* practice demonstrated by Miura Sensei which focused power at the conclusion of the cut driven by the breath, the *kiai*, or spirit shout, from the *hara*. The cut was efficient and effective. In Kyoto, I added to the basics that I had learned from Miura Sensei. And that is how it is. Nothing is ever finished.

"The Book of Water" includes all the specific instructions for the skills of kendo: bearing, stance, gaze, grip, footwork, attitude, approaches, timing, cuts, parries, communications. If I had done ten or fifty *suburi* per week in Hawaii, I did fifty to a hundred per day at Busen, just for warm-up. I made so many strikes that I forgot I was striking. Pushed physically beyond all thought and concept, the sword truly became an extension of my body just as the hand is an extension of the arm and taken completely for granted. It felt natural. If one thinks about the action, it interferes with the natural smooth and effective motion that, though not hurried, is quick.

At Busen, I learned *zanshin*, practiced best when exhaustion is so great that no more physical movement can be imagined. The literal translation for *zanshin* is "remaining spirit." No matter how conclusive a strike may be, whether on the battlefield or in a sports match where the final point is seemingly won, the kendoist must not quit. The kendoist is always prepared. The spirit must remain. The goal of training—the ten thousand, the one hundred thousand *suburi*—is to achieve spontaneity, to teach the body to act without thought. Always alert, always present, never overeager or uptight or assuming victory, *zanshin* as *kokoro ga nokoru* (the heart remains) is the essence of kendo spirit.

Zanshin can only occur when the sword and the swordsman are One (*itchi*), and sword actions are as natural as walking calmly and easily along a street. And so, we practiced and practiced and practiced some more at Busen. This I now realize was the wisdom of Ogawa Sensei requiring *kirikaeshi* (a drill involving a succession of strikes) for an hour a day for an entire year.

Zanshin is an essential aspect of the Nihon Kendo Kata. The *kata*, or forms, were a significant part of our practice. Not only do the forms use all of the techniques, but they also necessitate a relationship with the opponent as the kendo *kata* are always performed by two people. Usually, the sensei or the senior kendoist plays the "*Uchi Dachi*" and the student or less experienced kendoist plays the "*Shi Dachi*."

Discussions with my classmates were not abstract. When we ate together or had a few minutes of spare time, we would celebrate, drink sake, and talk kendo. But kendo talk was specific: how clever it had been to divert a *kote* hit with a feint and win with a *men* (the head as target) hit. The superior player opens and is missed only by inches when he goes for the *men*; he has to be very fast or be defeated at the *kote* (wrist) or *do* (the side of the chest).

Kendo training is about action, not thinking; thinking requires time and distance from the practice. When training, there is no room to think about yesterday or tomorrow, just this cut and that cut. When fighting, thinking will kill you. Despite the books written about kendo and other martial arts, words can only delude us into, at best, partial understanding. There is comprehension that one cannot put into words.

We practice, and that is a way of educating the body in action. Miyamoto Musashi stated that "you must study this well" as he writes about methods but always associates the "study" with comments such as: "You must train hard to understand it" and "With detailed practice you should be able to understand it." Yes, listen, reflect, and study, but it requires physical practice. With enough "doing," the *Do* (The Way) may become part of you.

At Busen, there was no time for book "study" of kendo. Our "study" of kendo was to watch, do, and do over and over again, training our bodies to have "muscle memory." Reflection is also a part of *budo* (The Way of the Warrior). But this would come, if ever, later. In fact, about fifty years later for me.

~

Finally, things were going well for me at Busen. I would have been in the thirty-first class, graduating in 1944. But that was not to be. In 1942, I was drafted into the Japanese military. Japan was at war, and many of the senseis and students had already been called to serve. There were only two entering classes after mine, and then Busen closed forever. Although the school itself was disbanded, the building where we practiced was eventually renovated and became a cultural treasure. It now serves as the venue for the annual Kyoto Taikai during Golden Week, the time between the late Emperor's birthday on April 29 and Boys' Day on May 5.

Farewell party with my Busen classmates when I was drafted into the Japanese Army. I am in the middle of the front row.

I received my draft notice during my second year of classes. Actually, attending Seiho Middle School for Japanese (*kokugo*) and then Ritsumeikan University for Chinese classical writing (*kanbun*) allowed me to remain out of service for longer than many of the other students at Busen. Each year, Ogawa Sensei submitted an exemption form for me, but my exemption finally expired. Because most of the senseis had already been drafted, there was certainly no excuse for me not to serve. Once notified, military service was mandatory.

As I waited for the inevitable day I would leave Busen to report to the army, I lived day to day. I didn't feel disloyal or even conflicted about serving in the Japanese army. To me it was just another war between two countries. Neither my classmates nor the Japanese authorities questioned whether I was loyal to the United States or Japan.

I don't recall political discussions among my classmates at Busen about going to war, but I do remember my going away party. We knew where I was going, and that those remaining would be following soon. What a grand celebration it was! We laughed and played and ate and drank until we were literally rolling on the floor, falling down laughing and dizzy with sake.

Probably because I was fluent in English and had relatives in Hawaii, the government decided not to send me to Tokyo to become an officer like my classmates. Although I served in the Japanese army from October 1942 to September 12, 1945, the end of World War II, I never fought directly or left the Japanese Mainland. It is likely that my Hawaiian background actually saved my life.

~

May 2004 marked the hundredth anniversary of Butoku Sai, a gathering in Kyoto of Butoku Kai, a group of elite martial artists from around the world. At that time, I was eighty-five years old and no longer able to travel. Most of my classmates from Busen were gone. Yet after all these years, I remembered each word of our school song, which was composed by Yabe Osamu of Ehime Prefecture, a student of the twenty-first graduating class in 1935.

Kanmu no mikado itsu kimasu
Miyai wa chikaki manabiya ni
Yamato gokoro wo iya migaku
Kore zo Busen no hokori naru

Meiyo renchi wo inochi to shi
Shitsu jitsu koken mune to shite
Hibi ni isoshimu shuyo wa
Warera kenji no tsutome zoya

Tagai ni kitou tetsu wan ni
Fukutsu no chisho atsuku moe
Yama o mo nukan sono iki wa
Hiroku tenka wo doyomosan

The rough translation of these verses is:

I'm proud to be learning and polishing
my *Yamato gokuro*, Japanese spirit,
at Busen, this institute of higher learning
located near the Heian Jingu shrine.
This is Busen's pride.

It is our duty to diligently and vigorously train daily
to forge and temper our bodies and spirit
together with honor, grace, and simplicity.

The world will sense that we have a tremendous force
that never quits, the power to move mountains
that will result in calming the world.

I sang our school song in Japanese for my few remaining classmates from Busen and recorded it on videotape. In that way, despite all my years in the United States, I was able to be with them as they celebrated and grieved. I am Japanese in spirit even though I know a wider world. I love the plumeria and gentle breezes of my boyhood in Hawaii as well as the cherry blossoms of Japan.

3
Fire
火

The true Way of strategy is the craft of defeating the enemy in a fight, and nothing other than this. If you attain and adhere to the wisdom of my strategy, you need never doubt that you will win.

—Miyamoto Musashi

As I begin this chapter, I recall the Nisei song composed by one of the Japanese language teachers at the Wahiawa Hongwanji Buddhist temple. He based it on an old Japanese school song and adapted the words to our life in Hawaii. We all knew the song and sang it almost as what would be called a pep rally song today. I recently recorded it:

Rekishi wa nagashi sanzen nen
Koto kagayaku hinomoto
No fubo no chi ukeshi warera nari
Seigi wo motte kuni wo tate
Sekai ni kan taru tomi wo motsu
Amerika shimin no warera nari

Roughly translated, it means:

Long three-thousand-year history,
Of the shining unbroken Japanese Imperial line.

We, the heirs of this three-thousand-year lineage,
With justice we build this country,
A nation unsurpassed in the world, as ours.
American citizens we became.

My brother, Brian, and me (in the Busen uniform) in 1941.

I don't know what my father thought about the Japanese attack on Pearl Harbor on December 7, 1941, but I do know that after my brother, Tomio (Brian), graduated from high school in 1941, he sent him to Japan, knowing that he would be drafted into the Japanese Imperial Army. When Brian arrived in Kyoto, I saw him for one day; the next he answered the draft. He fought in the Japan-China War, which began in 1931 with the invasion of Manchuria. His was a gentler nature than mine when we were kids in Wahiawa, so I doubt that Brian was eager to be a soldier. But he had no choice. He had to obey our father.

In later years, Brian spoke of his war experience rarely, but I know his time in service was not easy. He was pure Japanese, but having been raised in Hawaii, his language skills were even more lacking than mine when I arrived at Kyoto. A worthy Japanese does not speak pidgin. His fellow soldiers not only rejected him but beat him frequently. The Japanese invasion of China brought hell for the Chinese but also for my brother, and the Japanese Army brought him nothing but a constant, tortuous hell.

Although my father had lived in Hawaii since he was a young man, he always considered himself Japanese. During the War, still living in Hawaii, he was threatened with prison by the US authorities. But not for long. My two eldest sisters were nurses, and their contributions were needed desperately in the hospitals filled with wounded soldiers. They threatened to quit if he were jailed. Their nursing skills trumped any perceived threat from my father, and he returned home. His longing for Japan, and his wish to die in his homeland, was finally realized after the War, when he returned to his ancestral lands in Kure, leaving my mother behind. He lived there until he died in his late seventies in the 1960s.

In Japan, when a man went to war, it was assumed he would die, not that he might die. That is something to ponder well, so I'll say it again: "In Japan, when a man went to war, it was assumed he would die." The samurai warrior of old considered himself already dead, which enabled him to be clear and calm in any situation. I know that because I am a human being, I will die. But because I am a human being, like all human beings, I don't want to die. I don't know when or under what circumstances I will die, but as I was a soldier, I knew I would likely die sooner rather than later. This is a fact. In Japanese, we say, *mono no aware*, the realization of being human. This is an acceptance. I accepted my fate and believed that when death came, I would die with honor.

That was part of being a traditional Japanese, and Busen was certainly traditional. It is said that the sword and the brush—and the cherry blossom—reflect the soul of Japan. This is a soul that is reflective of nature, knowing that all who live must die, but that while living, life can be contemplative, discerning, and beautiful. These natural qualities form the ideals of martial arts, which emphasize skill but also wisdom, harmony, and serenity. This is *Yamato* (Japan) *damashii* (soul).

Yamato-damashii is a difficult concept to explain. It is a term indicative of the people's will. It is the fighting spirit of the Japanese soldier. But it is not just a fighting spirit. It is part of the great soul of the people, tied to the very origins of the Japanese. When I was at Busen, *Yamato-damashii* spirit was very much alive. The Emperor was the spiritual head of Japan. Japanese believed the Emperor was descended from the gods through an unbroken line of descent, and many could cite the whole lineage. No one questioned any sacrifice required by the gods or the Emperor. Like a father with his children, the Emperor's love for his people and theirs for him was sacred. As a Japanese son would not disobey his father, so the Japanese people would not disobey their Emperor.

If I were pushed to define *Yamato-damashii*, my response would be a comparison to the cherry blossom. It blooms abundantly for a brief moment, and then flutters down with no regret. That is how the brave Japanese should be.

Shikishima no
Yamato gokoro wo
hito towaba

Asahi ni niou
Yama zakura kana

Of a thousand islands
Japanese heart is

the fragrance in the morning sun
of the mountain cherry blossom

In 1998, long after the War had ended, I received a letter from Tomano Kenzan (Keitaro), a famous artist in Osaka, who recalled the story of an Australian Navy general. The general gave a memorial service from a podium draped with an Australian flag for a brave Japanese soldier who had tried to bomb an Australian warship from a suicide submarine. The general spoke with the mother of the soldier and was moved by the young man's bravery, even though he was the enemy, and even more by the bravery of his mother, who assumed her son would die. He learned a lesson, he said, from the enemy and began to understand much of the Japanese spirit from Mother Matsue's bittersweet *waka*, a poem with a syllable pattern of 5-7-5-7-7.

Kimi ga tame
Shine to sodateshi
Hana naredo
Arashi no ato no
Niwa sabishi kere

For the Emperor,
I raised you to die
like a cherry blossom.
Yet after the storm
how lonesome my yard.

~

As I left Kyoto early on the morning after my send-off party, I longed to return to Hawaii, but instead I traveled to my paternal grandfather's house in Hayashiyama (now Miharashi Cho) in Kure, Hiroshima Prefecture. Although I was born in Wahiawa, Hawaii, in the official Japanese family register (the *koseki tohon*), I am registered in Hiroshima-ken, Kure-shi. Therefore, I had to depart for the military from Kure. My trip to Kure was not for family goodbye parties or last farewells. In fact, I had never met my grandfather before that day. I walked to the farm in the early afternoon, and my grandfather, Omoto Umenosuke, fondly called Omoto No Ojii-chan (Grandpa Omoto) by his neighbors, was working in the rice paddy by the sea. He looked up, slowly walked toward me across the terraced vegetable patches, wearing straw sandals, his shoulders slightly stooped, his head covered by a straw hat. We bowed, and he said, "Nobuto?" He seemed to know me, but whether he was expecting me or not, I don't know.

Most of the neighbors were my father's brothers and sisters. I recognized them because they looked like my father, so maybe I looked like my father and that is how my grandfather recognized me. He led me to his hundred-year-old two-room house with no running water, a Japanese deep bathtub, an attached outhouse, and one dangling electric light that lacked a light bulb. He nodded toward a corner for me to deposit my pack. He then made tea, and we drank together, quietly. He knew why I was there, and he was a man of few words. Then he returned to the rice paddy.

I followed and worked beside him until sundown. We returned, and he gave me rice with bits of fish. The fishermen in the village threw a few small fish on the beach, knowing he would gather them for his meal. He never bought anything but sake, which we drank together before sleeping. He lit a lantern, chanted the Shoshinge, the chant of True Faith of Jodo Shinshu Buddhism, before the *butsudan* (a Buddhist altar), and we slept. At dawn the next morning, after he chanted Shoshinge, we boiled water drawn from the cistern to cook the rice and make tea. After breakfast, he returned to the fields, and I walked to town to register with the Army. The next day I left for Hiroshima for basic training.

The training in Japanese boot camp was rough. It was designed to turn a man into a fighting machine, to make him tough. Soldiers were made to run until they dropped and then told to run some more. There was no sympathy for the recruits, for there is no sympathy in war, no excuses or escapes. If a man fell, he was pushed up and received a *binta* (hard smack) as punishment and was often assigned extra physical tasks. Also, the trainees were often harassed. Even if a futon was laid out perfectly, an officer might throw it apart and require it to be redone. Men who complained were taunted as being *monkus* (whiners). To get used to punishment, soldiers were punished. Orders needed to be followed without question, no matter how seemingly absurd or inhumane. We practiced against straw enemies consisting of bodies without faces, or paper targets with demonic faces. If a soldier hesitates before attacking, it can be a matter of life or death.

The *budo* philosophy focuses training equally on mental strength so that actual physical contact often becomes unnecessary. But the physical and mental pressures are similar. For me, because of all the challenges I faced in Kyoto—the mental pressure of trying to learn to speak, read, and write the Japanese language; doing household tasks for Ogawa Sensei and his children; and the physical training at Busen—Japanese boot camp seemed easy. In fact, I had to learn to be tough even when I was on the Seiho High School kendo team. If we won, our instructor, Tanaka Tomoharu Tomokazu "Chiichi" Sensei, would shout, "That's not the way to win!" and whack us on the rear end with chunks of firewood. Chiichi Sensei had formerly served in the Japanese Army, as had other instructors at Busen, and they brought military discipline to the team. "*Urusai na! Gamanshiro!*" "Shut up! Take the pain!" I learned that strength is not only in giving a punch but also in taking a punch.

Boot camp trained soldiers in the use of weaponry. I had learned this at Busen. I was especially good at *juken jutsu,* bayonet. The Principal of Busen was General Hayashi Senjuro. As in any school, he administered all the departments, but he was especially enthusiastic for *juken jutsu,* and those of us in the kendo and judo sections of Busen were offered the training. "Offer" and "volunteer" at Busen, however, were generally considered commands, especially for the kendo students, who enjoyed higher status. At Busen, *juken jutsu,* which used a wooden training rifle in place of a bayonet, was taught by one of the general's sergeants as a practical military skill.

During boot camp, I beat everyone, even the instructors, with the bayonet. Between deployments, I also enjoyed bayonet and sword "play" practice at the base in Hiroshima. The *waza,* or techniques, of kendo training were not only applicable during basic training but assured success against opponents. The samurai sword was modified for the army, a *gunto,* or military sword, which was used for ritual and saluting. We also trained with guns and rifles.

Nevertheless, I was not assigned to a cadet group, where all the other college students were placed. After basic training, the cadets were sent to Tokyo for officer training after which they returned as *Minarai Shikan* (apprentice officers). Since I was only a sergeant, I had to salute them even though I could whip them at bayonet practice. I was angry when I had to salute those less talented officers; nonetheless, I followed military training and saluted. After apprenticeship, when they achieved the rank of second lieutenant, they were all sent to combat. Few returned.

I was the only former college student stationed in Hiroshima and assigned to the Transportation Corps, certainly not considered a prestigious assignment. Combat is always the way of advancement in the military, not the motor pool. The *Shichotai* (Transportation Corps) was my home base for three years, and I never experienced combat. The base was located about a thousand yards from the atomic bomb ground zero.

I was sent to the Tokyo Tank School for about six months to learn how to operate tanks and how to dismantle and reassemble them. We also learned to attack tanks with yellow bombs (*oh shoku yaku)* that we carried under our arms, and we were taught how to jump right into the wheels of the tanks if necessary, destroying both the tank and us.

Seppuku, the ritual suicide samurais performed by ceremoniously cutting open the *hara* with the sword, was the honorable way to die for the Emperor. Reasons for *seppuku* included failure or defeat in battle. The slang term *harakiri* (literally, gut cutting), coined by the West during World War II, debases the conscious will and courage implicit in the traditional concept. Nonetheless, the average soldier needs to be honored, even if his suicide was not so pure as that of the samurai.

Tradition required one to die honorably by *seppuku* for one's mistake or disgraceful act. But Ogawa Kinnosuke Sensei, my teacher and mentor at Busen, told me that modern kendo did not require *seppuku*. "If you make a mistake or commit a disgraceful act, Omoto, live as long as you can. You can't recover the mistakes you made, but value yourself and show your bravery and repentance by being useful to your neighbors and the world for as long as you live." My modern kendo spirit, modern *bushido*, or Hawaiian Yamato spirit, would not allow me to commit suicide, but rather survive to throw more bombs. I would fight to live and live to fight more.

Would I have committed suicide if I could not imagine an alternative or had been ordered to, as were the kamikaze pilots? I have to answer that I don't know. Luckily, I did not have to face that decision, but it is likely that if the order had been issued, I would have complied and thereby at least died honorably. Either way I would have been dead. In the Japanese military, to refuse an order is treason, punishable by death. However, war is about death. War means blood and pain—death. That is the bottom line. If you are a foot soldier in close combat, survival is a matter of luck, or perhaps karma.

So it proved for me. The day I left Tokyo, I learned that the tank school had been bombed. There were few, if any, survivors. To survive by hours was my karma. It had no relationship to my kendo training or personal control. I was lucky for my order to depart, just as I would have been unlucky to be ordered to stay at the school another day or to sacrifice myself.

My next assignment was for horse and buggy training at Kumamoto Castle, located on the southern island of Kyushu and noted for its mountains, beautiful gardens, and history. This is the area where Miyamoto Musashi spent his last days and wrote *The Book of Five Rings*. I especially enjoyed this assignment.

In 1640, when Musashi was fifty-six years old, after his sixth and final battle during the siege of Shimabara in 1637, he took up residence at Kumamoto as a guest of Lord Hosokawa Tadatoshi. He was given the rank of general of a division. Here he participated in his last, and as always, victorious duel, and then he took residence in the old castle of Chiba, adjacent to Kumamoto Castle. He spent most of his time practicing the arts of calligraphy, painting, and tea ceremony. Shaken by the death of

Lord Hosokawa in 1641, he retreated to fulfill the Lord's command to explain the ideas of his strategy that had guided his life as a samurai. In 1643, at fifty-nine years old, Musashi departed for Mount Iwato, located about twelve kilometers southwest of Kumamoto, where he lived in Reigando (spirit rock) Cave. Here he remained and wrote the *Gorin no Sho* (*The Book of Five Rings*). He died at the age of sixty-one in 1645.

All kendoists and most Japanese know and revere Musashi, but I had not yet penetrated more than about twelve pages of the copy of the *Gorin no Sho* in the book called *Kendo* by Takao Sasaburo that was given to me by Miura Sensei when I left for Japan. And here I was in Kumamoto with no time for sightseeing or study. Even a fool could appreciate the exquisite natural beauty of the surroundings.

For our morning training, we would run three miles to Suizenji Park, a thoroughly pleasant exercise. Then we learned how to dismantle buggies and cannons, pack them onto horses, and transport the parts into the hills, where they would be reassembled. I groomed, fed, and cared for the horses. Being with the horses was my favorite duty. I respected the horses and gained their trust, just as my father had in his work as a blacksmith in Wahiawa. A quiet spirit is necessary as the horse can feel fear and will respond with fear by kicking or rearing or refusing to be still. During the cold winter, I snuggled with the horses and was saved from freezing. The horses had moist warmth and shared their flanks with me.

Kendo training helped me with the horses, something I would never have anticipated. Miyamoto Musashi taught that "Both in fighting and in everyday life you should be determined though calm. Meet the situation without tenseness yet not recklessly, your spirit settled yet unbiased." Every practice begins and ends with *meiso*, (a meditation done with the hands facing upward). Generally, the meditation period is brief, only a few minutes, but that is time enough to leave behind all other concerns, leaving the mind open and allowing the spirit to settle and quiet. I later realized that my response to the horses reflected Takano Sasaburo attitude on relationships, which was part of my body's knowledge, between *uchi tachi* and *shi tachi* in *kata*.

At Busen, we also learned the kendo gaze. Described by Musashi, the gaze is twofold: perception and sight. "It is important to see distant things as if they were close and to take a distanced view of close things . . . to look to both sides without moving the eyes." Thus, the gaze is large and broad. So when I approached the horses, I was calm. I respected their power and their intelligence. I spoke to them softly, and noting how they communicated with each other by sharing breath, I breathed into their nostrils. I did not stare into their eyes, which I now understand can both frighten and challenge them. My gaze was perception, not challenge. The horses acknowledged this attitude and reflected it back to me. But food helped. When I could, I fed them their favorite foods, apples and carrots. I loved the horses, and for about six months, I actually enjoyed my training at Kumamoto, unlike the other soldiers who never slept with the horses.

After my horse and buggy training, I was sent back to Hiroshima, where I was designated *Minarai Shikan*, a graduate of military war school. I don't know why. Promotion just happened in the Japanese army. It was not necessarily connected to time in service or aptitude. An officer said I was *Minarai Shikan*, and so I was. At a young age, I came to appreciate the random nature of our lives.

As an officer, I was put in charge of training new troops. They were young, too young in fact. Teenagers were called to fill the need for more soldiers. And because they were young, they were not only vigorous but also cocky. One day I was running in the lead during our morning exercises. One of the sergeants informed me that some recruits were complaining that it wasn't fair that Omoto *Minarai Shikan* carried only a light sword, but the recruits had to carry heavy rifles and machine guns.

The next day, immediately after leaving the barracks, I yelled "*Kake Ashi!*" ("Run!"). Give me your machine gun and follow me." We ran at full speed. I left one soldier, a sergeant, to follow at the rear and pick up all those who dropped out. By the end of the training run, many of the young kids had dropped out. I was never criticized again. And they had learned a lesson. There is a Japanese doll, the Daruma. Knock it down, and it comes back up. There is an old Japanese saying, "*Nan na korobi ya oki.*" It means "Seven times knocked down, get up on the eighth!" This is the way of the soldier, but when soldiers are still children, it is a difficult requirement. My kendo training helped me to endure. I had learned about "intent," to firmly focus only upon the present task, to firmly commit with absolute resolve, and thereby to win. And with meditation, I knew how to refresh my body, to relax and recuperate.

My next assignment was to learn to operate and repair Toyota six-cylinder trucks. This was easy for me. As a boy growing up in Hawaii, I had worked with my father, who was a blacksmith. He also repaired all parts of the Model T Ford and modified other sedans to use as cooler trucks for fruit, vegetable, and fresh fish peddlers, so I was familiar with mechanical repairs. After basic learning, I was sent on a winter convoy (*jidosha taikan kogun*) for more truck experience. After traveling for three days on the long convoy route through the remote countryside of Hiroshima, we stopped near a large brewery, where huge tubs of sake were stored. This became a great celebration. Our spirits were lifted by a party; that cold evening we were warmed by sake in a brief respite from the harshness of life as soldiers. Our rations provided basic nutrition but did not include sake. Parties or R & R leave were not a part of Japanese military training.

The next morning, after filling our canteens with sake instead of water, we continued our travel. It was my turn to be flag man, moving between the trucks to communicate distances and road conditions to the truck in the rear. At the time, I didn't think I was lucky to pull this duty because it was cold, and all the other soldiers were under the canvas, taking it easy with sake-filled canteens. The trucks were loaded with three fifty-gallon drums filled with fuel alcohol because Japan had almost completely run out of gasoline. Certainly, none could be spared for military exercises.

As we were slowly moving on a narrow snow-covered road, my truck started to skid toward the left side. All of a sudden, the left front wheel ran off the road and started tipping over a cliff. Instinctively, I put my hands on the rail on the right side and somersaulted onto the road out of the path of the truck. I desperately tried to hang onto the edge of the road but failed and started sliding down a steep cliff until I caught a branch of a small tree about midway between the road and a rice paddy at least thirty feet below. I suffered scratches and bruises. Everyone inside was crushed by the truck and the fifty-gallon fuel drums. Many hours later, an ambulance arrived at the scene. Not only did I survive the plunge, but as a bonus, I got a ride on a stretcher to the ambulance and safety.

Sometimes I wonder whether my reflexive response in this emergency was due to kendo training. Kendo is all about offensive resolute action. Training hones the reflexes so that action is instantaneous, without thought. The greatest risk comes with hesitation, when one briefly loses his nerve. Survival depends on boldness. I had, of course, learned the strategy of examining my environment and was aware of the cliff. I was also in good physical shape. But without kendo training, I'm not sure my response would have been quick enough to save my life.

There are other times, however, when action is not the best approach. When I returned to Hiroshima, I was assigned to air-raid watch as a lookout on top of a roof. As always, I considered my surroundings. Our base was darkened to avoid being identified as a target. A group of American bombers flew over my head almost close enough to touch. I didn't shoot. Had I done so, the entire barracks area would have been discovered and bombed. But it might have been destroyed anyway if we had already been noted as the target. In that case, if I had survived, I would have been held responsible for not alerting our defenses and likely executed. Certainly, I would have been utterly disgraced. Again, I was very lucky because there was another, completely unacceptable reason that I didn't shoot. I knew that Walter, my childhood friend in Hawaii, and other friends I had grown up with were all fighting on the American side. I wondered if I had shot, would I have killed Walter or one of my other friends? I couldn't shoot. I would rather have been shamed and executed. I could never have lived knowing I had killed one of my friends, even if from a distance in modern warfare. To have killed Walter would have destroyed my spirit and made life unbearable. Boot camp training does not teach one how to deal with such regret.

When I returned to Kochi, I trained more new recruits. But this time, instead of young boys, they were old, feeble men, often disabled and sick. All the college students and young men had already been drafted, leaving only the "Han" squad, these sad old men. The Japanese army was obviously in poor condition, and it was becoming apparent that Japan was losing the war. These old soldiers were throwaway men.

I thought that training these old people to fight, some of whom actually belonged in a nursing home, was absurd, a waste of energy, and cruel. So I gave them time to rest and recuperate. I would lead them out of the barracks with great gusto for training, but as we approached the training field, we just lay down and rested. If I had been caught doing this, I would have been court-martialed. But I guess the happy-go-lucky Hawaiian boy had emerged, and I thought, "What the heck! These old people can't fight. They need rest more than anything else to merely survive."

I felt very sorry for the old soldiers. Once an intake sergeant came to me with a picture of a lady. He said one of the old soldiers who had just been inducted a couple of days before had the photograph in his wallet. It was typical that the old soldiers were harassed for trivial things. To try to "shape them up," they were given a *binta*, a hard whack on both sides of the face. But I felt that confiscating this picture was psychological cruelty. I called for the old man and asked him to identify the lady. "My wife," he answered softly, shaking because he thought I would give him another *binta*. "Okay," I said. "Put this back in your wallet and go back to your bunk." Then I called the soldier who had taken the picture from the old man. I reprimanded him and came close to calling him a bully. "Don't do that to the soldiers. They have the right to carry their wives' pictures in their wallets," I barked. "And before you give *binta* to any of them, see me first. I want to know why, and it better be a good reason!" Long after the War, when I was living in Matsue, the capital city of Shimane Prefecture, located on the Sea of Japan, this nameless old soldier found me and came to thank me.

In the early spring of 1945, I had full responsibility for the welfare of my troops. All were novices, the very young and the elderly. My troop consisted of four six-cylinder Toyota trucks, and four squads, a total of eighteen soldiers, including two sergeants, a driver, an assistant, and two flaggers. We were assigned to serve in Kochi City in Kochi Prefecture on Shikoku Island. We rarely stayed in the city, however, and usually camped in scattered places on the hillside surrounding the city.

Our mission was tough, beginning before dawn and ending late at night. Some days we worked around the clock. Our rations were minimal, and we were always hungry, but we kept on moving and rested only when we were completely exhausted. We cut and loaded logs from the mountains onto the trucks with no towing tools of any kind and then hauled them to the Kochi shoreline to furnish materials for the barricades the infantry soldiers were building to protect the Japanese Mainland from invasion. The Allies were at our borders. On the return trip, we hauled food and supplies from the Kochi warehouse for redistribution to the farmers' warehouses located throughout the hills. Food was critical and, in this way, we distributed the supplies over a larger area to avoid losing everything to bombs.

We kept moving through the dark one night, long after we all wanted and desperately needed to rest. One of the sergeants asked me to allow the soldiers to sleep in the shoreline warehouse, where we had stopped for a few minutes after loading for the return trip.

The warehouse was now half empty and seemed luxurious compared to our usual sleeping conditions. I rejected the request, fearing that the warehouse might be a target, and after a rest of only a few minutes, I started up the hill with very unhappy soldiers. About halfway up the hill, we heard B-52 bombers flying over very high, but they didn't drop any bombs. "Turn off the lights," I ordered, "and sleep right where you are!" Shortly thereafter, from way out in the Pacific, a swarm of P-51s sprayed some kind of liquid flame accelerant on the Kochi warehouse. Then the second line dropped flare bombs. In seconds, the entire warehouse exploded, lighting the shoreline of Kochi. They ignored our little convoy, or perhaps never spotted us. No one complained about lack of sleep that night! Once again, luck was with me.

My final order was to return to Kochi to gather the supplies we had saved by storing them in farmers' warehouses in the hills. The roads were narrow, the drivers inexperienced, and the trucks easily slid into the rice paddies. We had no towing tools so when a truck was stuck, everyone would work together to heave the truck upright and attempt to get it back on the road. But that was easy compared to rescuing our own men, who would often become trapped inside the truck when it rolled. One time a truck rolled over and pinned a soldier underneath. Gasoline spilled from the truck and covered his body. We finally rolled the truck off him, but he was in no shape to continue his duties. Due to the gasoline burns, his skin was peeling from his entire body. He suffered horribly, especially when he moved. I sent him back to Hiroshima. Then came the atomic bomb, which released his pain completely.

How perfunctory and cold my attitude now seems—he burned, then died. No description of his unrelenting screams of agony, his cries to his mother, the terror in his eyes. But that is what happens in war. Too much suffering and death can drive a man insane unless the senses of pity and horror are numbed. Anger is acceptable. Soldiers are taught not to look in the eyes of an enemy when being asked to kill in close combat. Looking into the eyes creates a relationship. We are taught about relationship in kendo. But there is no time in boot camp to learn how to create a life as well as take a life. In modern warfare, killing is, when possible, more distant. That is probably good for the mental health of soldiers even though it avoids confronting the reality of death on a bloody battlefield.

~

We were so isolated in Kochi that we had lost communications with our base in Hiroshima. We didn't know about the Bomb or the end of the War until a few weeks after Japan surrendered. But we weren't surprised. The old soldiers were tired and already felt defeated, and most of us had known for some months that the war was lost. We just didn't know the form that loss would take.

We arrived back in Hiroshima, completely unprepared for the devastation. We skirted the city. Schichotai, our base, had been evaporated. There are no words for what we saw. A bomb, yes, but what kind of a bomb? Annihilation of this magnitude was inconceivable! And the devastation assaulted us wherever we gazed.

Burned remains of Schichotai, the transport base in Hiroshima, where I had been stationed.

The central city was flattened. Only the skeleton of a few brick buildings to the west remained. Two hundred thousand people died after the initial explosion. The sky was still thick with smoke from smoldering buildings and funeral pyres. Bodies could no longer be cremated separately with respect and proper ritual but were stacked in piles for mass disposal. There was no ability to dignify death at this scale. Bodies were everywhere, horribly maimed and decaying, magnets for millions of flies. And there were the injured and dying, waiting and hoping for help. The city was eerily quiet. The sobs and screams of children occasionally pierced the silence, but adults didn't speak. What could be said? People continued to die. But there were no words.

There was no time for mourning. There was little food. Drinking water was scarce since the rivers weaving through the city were contaminated with dead bodies and the fallout from the bomb. There were too few doctors. There was neither help nor medical supplies. Shock and suffering, chaos and destruction . . .

Of course, we soldiers, like the citizens of Hiroshima and the military leaders, did not know the nature of the bomb, only rumors. Many had heard the Emperor's surrender speech, the first time he had spoken on the radio but in a language that common people had difficulty understanding. A joint Army-Navy meeting on August 10, 1945, under the auspices of the Imperial Headquarters, confirmed that the Americans had dropped an atomic bomb. But information filtered to the people more slowly, and it was more than a week before most Japanese heard the truth. Even then, it was almost impossible to understand. There was no comprehension and certainly no knowledge of the long-term effects of radiation. Moreover, the Allied Occupation General Headquarters (GHQ) issued a press code on September 19, restricting references to the atomic bomb in speech, reporting, and publications. GHQ had to give permission, and generally refused, prohibiting any publication of information about the A-bomb.

Kendo training teaches us to not be afraid. Fear alters the body, creating tension and compromising one's response. Kendo training failed me at Hiroshima. This was a world gone mad, pure destruction, and I felt a deep, dark, paralyzing fear beyond reason or action. But maybe my training did help a bit because I remembered to breathe deeply, five meditative breaths to the *hara*, and regained some calm. At the Hiroshima railroad station, where no trains were now being dispatched, I turned to my soldiers and asked if they had a home. Their replies were immediate. "*Hai! Hai! Hai!*" Everyone had a home. "Go," I said, and they all started walking toward home.

Then I realized I was alone. Did I have a home I could return to? The question was empty, an echo from nowhere. I had no home. I longed for Hawaii, but it was impossible for me to return. Wahiawa was where I longed to be, in the gentle islands smelling of plumeria and wild ginger. Even rotting mangoes have a fecund, sweet smell. All I could smell here was burnt flesh, a smell that I tried to forget. In fact, I have tried to forget everything about Hiroshima after the Bomb.

During the times when I was nearly killed, I lost the capacity for fear. No flinching, no jumpiness. Instinct took over; no thoughts of terrible possibilities or hopes for the future or even of dying. I just blocked everything. The War was finished, but war is never finished just because one side surrenders. Hiroshima is proof of that. I turned toward Kure and my grandfather's house. There was no other choice. I didn't know whether the house was even still there. But I was lucky. I was alive, not injured, and I had to respect this life I was given and get up, move, act.

I set out alone from Hiroshima Station on the long, mountainous walk to Kure. All I had was my soldier's uniform to cover my skin, a military backpack, and my Japanese sword hanging from my left side. I didn't know whether I would get there or not. I didn't care. I just walked at a slow pace, chewing on the remains of hard crackers, the only food I had, and soon they were gone. I had no water. And Hiroshima in August is hot and humid.

I was thirsty and hungry. When I saw a green plant along the road, although most often it was only a blade of grass, I ate it. Fasting is said to enhance clarity. Perhaps, but starvation is just painful. I understood hunger. The gut feels like it is ripping apart, twisted and stretched. All I could think of was food, and then nothing. I just put one foot in front of the other.

The road was full of other soldiers and entire families leaving Hiroshima. There was no food for any of us. We were all helpless. We were all in rags. Nobody was in any position to give help.

There was no shelter. People slept by the side of the road, under rags or in lean-tos made of debris or pieces of metal. Abandoned vehicles gave some respite. It was cold at night, boiling during the day. At times it rained, at times the wind blew, but there was no shelter.

I turned east toward the shores between Hiroshima and Kure. There I found seaweed, clams, and some small fish. I scooped them up with both hands and stuffed them into my mouth, whole and raw. I ate everything raw. I told myself, "If they move, eat 'em." Living creatures are either prey or predator. I would live, but I no longer cared. Walk, walk, walk. Continuing to walk but no longer caring whether I got to Kure or not. One foot at a time. Walking, walking . . .

4
Wind
風

To renew, when we are deadlocked with the enemy, means that without changing our circumstances, we change our spirit and win through a different technique.

—Miyamoto Musashi

I DON'T REMEMBER HOW MANY DAYS it took me to reach Hayashi Yama (now Miharashi Cho), my grandfather's village in Kure, but when I finally looked up, it was sunrise, and I saw my grandfather working in the fields just as he had been doing when I left for the Army that morning in 1942. Unlike the fifteen million homeless people throughout Japan, I had a home to live in and some food. But nothing was the same.

My grandfather had always been a poor farmer, but now he had only a small garden, where he grew potatoes, yams, soybeans, and turnips. His rice field had been filled in by the Japanese army to construct a two-story barracks for the soldiers. Hastily built, unlike the little two-room house built by my great-grandfather more than a hundred years ago, the building had already started to fall apart. The barracks building was useless now, but, even more significant, the rice field had been destroyed. This field had not only supported my grandfather but also helped to provide food for eight other relatives and their families living next door and throughout the hills surrounding my grandfather's house.

My father used to say that if you put energy into planting seeds, probably you'd have a harvest. But if you're lazy and don't plant anything, there won't be any possibility of a harvest. Remembering my father's words, every day I worked to reclaim the rice field. First, I moved the wood from the old barracks into a pile, and then the long task of clearing the dirt began.

The Army had covered the low, wet field with about three feet of hard packed sand and dirt. There were no tools for dirt clearing, so I used garden tools. After filling an old wheelbarrow with a load of dirt, I pushed it up the hill, dumped it, and started again. Every day I hauled until there was a small area restored to plant a little rice. This was a start, and after a few months, I had cleared about an acre. But seeds were scarce, and what seeds we could find seemed to grow very slowly. Meanwhile, hunger didn't wait; everyone needed more rice.

There was a salt shortage in Japan, so we made our own salt from the sea. First, I found a sheet of galvanized tin and made a square frying pan out of it by bending the four sides. Next I put it on some rocks to create an open space underneath it. Then I hauled seawater from about thirty yards away with a clean new honey bucket on each end of a pole. I had to make several trips with the pole balanced on my shoulder. Fortunately, I had ample wood to burn from the old Japanese army barracks. But it took quite a while to boil down enough seawater to produce salt. We used some of this salt ourselves and bartered or sold the rest.

We had food, but not enough. The whole family, including my aunts and uncles, shared whatever was available. Sometimes there was only one bowl of rice for each person for an entire week. We added vegetables from the small garden to the rice and usually added weeds as well. We also traded some of our vegetables for barley. Fish were scarce because most of the fishermen had been drafted and were now dead, and the sea had been contaminated by fuel oil and war debris. The small fish that had been left on the beach for my grandfather before the war were now rare.

Gathering food in Hayashi Yama was not so different from what I had done when I walked from Hiroshima to Kure, when anything that moved in the sea or on land became food. My aunts traded their silk kimonos and obis for rice. Often, they walked miles to barter, but returned with handfuls of rice at best. We were hungry, but we didn't starve.

Despite our hunger, my grandfather continued to save rice to place into the three cone-shaped containers for the *butsudan*. Now, however, he placed only a few grains of rice in each container and, with a shaking hand, slid the containers into the curved slots in the center, carefully placing them on each side of the altar. As he had always done, he then took out the lacquered black box from the altar drawer, which contained his one book, opened to the Shoshinge page, and began to chant. He had the whole book memorized, but to learn, I would follow the words as he turned the pages of the book. I noticed that often he was not chanting the words that were printed on the opened page. When I asked him about this, he nodded and said, "*Kamawan*" ("That's okay") and continued chanting. I realized from my grandfather that intent is as important as correctness. It is not the practice of reading, but the quality of the practice that gives energy to the spirit by doing it every day. It is not so much "what" you do as "how" you do it.

During the day, we worked side by side. He worked as hard as I did—maybe harder because he was at least eighty years old. To plow the land, he tied the end of the wooden pick with a straw rope and then tied the other end across his back. Then he pounded the pick into the ground and pulled it with his body. He did not have enough strength to pull it with his hands. Every evening after work, he cooked whatever we had in a kettle of water over a small fire heated by the wood he gathered nearby. He didn't want help cooking and told me to sit near the hearth and watch.

My jobs were mostly carrying dirt, water, and "honey." I carried cold spring water in clean water buckets on my shoulders from the well and poured it into a five-gallon ceramic tub in the kitchen. The well was located about one block down a steep hill. It was easy going down but exhausting coming up. And a lot of water was needed, not only for cooking but also for bathing. The water would be poured into a cast iron, one-person tub, and then heated with wood, leaves, and twigs gathered from the forest or wood from the debris of the barracks. Everyone bathed before me, and by the time it was my turn, the water was neither warm nor clean. But it didn't matter. The only clothes I had were my Japanese Army uniform, which by then was permanently soiled.

I also collected the filled honey buckets from the outhouse and carried them on a wooden pole across my shoulders down the slope to the rice field. I recalled the man who collected "honey" in Kyoto. He was more skilled than I, but then I never thought I would do this job. The terraced hill was slippery, and sometimes I had to jump from one tier to a lower tier. It was difficult to keep my balance. When my bucket tilted, I was showered with raw honey. I still wore my tattered military uniform, and despite rinsing it in salt water, I smelled down to my bones for days.

Labor hard, eat little, fall into bed exhausted, and sleep. Life now was not much different than it had been at Busen or in the Army. However, the Army was more difficult for me because I didn't agree with the training. It was brutal. War is apt to bring out the worst qualities in men. Beating as a means of indoctrinating the recruits with the military spirit was a mistaken interpretation that perverted the samurai tradition. Without the *budo* spirit, routine beatings, if survived, merely instilled greater brutality in the trainees. Kendo training was tough, but part of a long tradition of training to be of service, not like the training that took place in boot camp. In the words of Miyamoto Musashi: "A thousand days of practice is forging and tempering your body and soul, and ten thousand days of practice is polishing the forged and tempered body and soul, while continuing to forge and temper."

At Busen, senior students would "shape up the underclassmen." The head of the senior class obtained permission from the principal, gathered the underclassman on the roof of the classroom building, and lectured the juniors, sophomores, and freshmen. We would have to listen, sitting in *seiza* (kneeling) position for two or more hours. Then each of the seniors would pick on an individual student, who had not bowed to the *sempai* on a particular day, and "Wham!" The student would get a *kiai*, or punch, to wake him up. It hurt. But he would not be repeatedly beaten, day after day, or with shoes and sticks, as happened with trainees in the Japanese Army. At Busen, the whack was not intended to be mean but rather a compassionate strike to remind you that you were at Busen, so you had to shape up and be alert. You must have *sen* (be one step ahead). Always, one step ahead in kendo and in life.

Naito Sensei, the first sensei at Busen, exemplified the life of kendo as the ethical principles of *budo*. He lived simply in an old house that he stubbornly refused to repair. Once a student, seeing the leaking roof, decided to help him by repairing his house. Naito Sensei acknowledged the student's attention but refused and then sent him away. During the freezing Kyoto winters, my own teacher, Ogawa Sensei, brushed his teeth in the snow and held winter practice, or *kangeiko*, in the unheated dojo. The true warrior (*bushi*) is selfless.

There is a story of a samurai who was hungry but gave his food to save a starving person. Then he pretended he had had a filling meal by picking his teeth with a toothpick. The life of kendo is to be tough but live kindly; to be fearless in battle; to be trustworthy; to polish yourself by taking care of both the body and the spirit; to not be a burden to others but rather to be of service to others in the community. If you want to be rich, don't bother with kendo.

My grandfather was not a kendoist, but he set an example of perseverance, kindness, and humility. He never complained, nor did I complain or feel anger while I lived with him.

I thought often during those bleak times of Ogawa Sensei's commentary on *seppuku*: "Live, don't die. Live long to contribute to others." Of course, I never went so far as contemplating suicide and often reminded myself how lucky I had been to escape death so many times in the Army and in Hiroshima. Everything after was a bonus. Nonetheless, negative emotions were hard to control, especially when I lived daily in an unhappy marriage.

~

Although I was married, I still worked for my grandfather clearing the rice fields, tearing down the barracks, and hauling the wood uphill. This was exhausting work, and dangerous. Once I fell through a hole on the second floor of the barracks but only suffered a few scrapes and bruises, so I continued working.

One day when an American walked by, I greeted him in English, and thus he discovered I was bilingual. In those days, interpreting jobs were in high demand. Captain Parker of the American Occupation Forces hired me, initially as a translator-interpreter.

When Captain Parker learned I could type, I became even more valuable as an employee because I could type the Japanese information directly without relying on a translator. I never would have thought that learning to type, which was a class I hated in the ninth grade at Leilehua High School, would become one of my assets for survival. Not only did I receive small payments from the Japanese government, but also, and much more importantly, Captain Parker gave me food. That was lucky because it meant the rice I received from my wife's family was no longer critical.

Captain Parker (photo provided by his widow, Mary Parker).

My wife's mother had a sharp eye and an even sharper tongue, and she resented anything I gave to my family. She brought rice from their farm in the country to our house in the village and thereby controlled exactly how much we received. She was much more my boss than the American soldiers I worked for. My wife obeyed her mother in all things and bossed me too. Neither respected me. I may have come from a farmer's family, but I wasn't a peasant! I had been a student at Busen, where I had assimilated the samurai culture. The War had prevented me from receiving positive recognition of the status I had worked so hard to achieve. Although I was no longer hungry, I was still seething with anger and resentment.

This all came to a head one hot summer day. My aunt and uncle wanted me to build them a large two-story house. Remembering how my grandfather had helped me after the War, I agreed to help my relatives.

One day when I was hauling the old lumber up the hill in preparation for construction, my wife called out and demanded to know what I was doing. When I said the house was for my aunt and uncle, she told me that I couldn't build a house for my relatives. Instead, it had to be for us alone. That was when I reached the breaking point! "Go home," I shouted and pointed to the door. "Go home to your mother! Now!!"

We never saw each other again. I added the divorce clause to the *koseki tohon*, the family registry required of all Japanese citizens. Thus, we were divorced. I had no regrets.

However, in the village at that time, divorce was not just a decision affecting the married couple but a matter of concern for the whole family. Not only was it considered a disgrace for the wife and her family but for the husband and his family as well. For years after the divorce, my wife's brother searched for me to right the wrong I had done to his sister and restore the family honor.

He caused me to move more than once. However, as divorce was handled in Japan in those days, the husband was considered to have all the power. The most direct impact of this unwritten law was that I received custody of my daughter, Miyuki, from my first marriage.

Before the divorce, my mother had spent about two weeks at my grandfather's house in Hayashi Yama, and she didn't like the way my wife and her mother bossed me. She did not criticize me for divorcing my wife.

But that was not the case with my father. Shortly before my divorce, he had returned to his beloved Japan and was also living in my grandfather's house. He felt that by divorcing my wife, I had stubbornly asserted my will and ignored custom. He was a stubborn man, and he renounced me. His rejection was more painful for me than my divorce.

The respect and duty (*oya ko ko*) owed to parents by their children is one of the traditional bonds in Japanese society. We are given life and receive our bodies from our parents, and their parents before them. Our parents and our ancestors live within us. Therefore, our bodies are gifts that we must care for, put to good use, and respect. It is our duty to stay healthy and be careful so our parents do not need to worry. We owe it to our parents to leave a good name for the next generation and to do well in school so that we can successfully contribute to the community. In brief, it is our duty to make our parents proud and to honor our ancestors. Of course, when the parents age, the duty is reversed. Old people must take the initiative to be healthy and continue to contribute. But if that is not possible, we care for our parents just as they cared for us as babies.

My father hoped I would return from Japan and become the sensei for all Japanese kendo in Hawaii. Now, I was a nobody, and I had sent my wife away, ignoring my father's wishes. When my father didn't respect my decision, I moved out of my grandfather's house.

"To hell with everything!" I said to myself. Everything—including regret, anxiety, hope, and even fear. I had no future. But I didn't pity myself. Never! I simply detached from everything.

This was a preview to lessons, with a more positive focus, I would later learn from Ono Sensei. After giving up, my luck improved.

~

After the divorce, I continued to work for the Japanese government and the Occupation Forces. Captain Parker was with the Army Counter Intelligence Corp (CIC). The perceived common enemy of both Japan and the United States was Communism, the Japanese Communist Party (JCP). Much of my work involved translating information provided by the Japanese police relevant to JCP movements. I translated the JCP newspaper, the *Akahata* (*Red Flag*) and police reports. My work was efficient because I directly typed raw information into English, unlike the other Japanese translators, who first laboriously wrote in long hand and then had to send the text to a typist.

Other security forces also employed me as a translator, including the British and the Australian and New Zealand Army Corps (ANZAC) in addition to the United States Army Criminal Investigation Division (CID) and the Air Force Office of Secret Investigation (OSI). These were forerunners for intelligence services like the CIA. I always kept my eyes and ears open but certainly was not like a spy character in a James Bond movie. Only once was I truly in danger.

After being employed by all the above organizations, I started working for the British Commonwealth Occupation Forces (BCOF) in Kure City. While continuing as an interpreter, my major job was as personnel manager for the Empire Club at Kure House. I worked there from about fall 1946 through about 1949. The Empire Club, which served all Occupation Forces personnel, was the center of activities and was open day and night to serve drinks, food, and snacks. Japanese nationals were hired as cashiers, waitresses, cooks, bakers, accountants, and janitors. There were also several translators on the floor to help interpret between the Occupation Forces managers and the Japanese employees.

Employees of the Empire Club.

As personnel manager, I hired the staff for the entire club. All across Japan, food was still scarce. The club was a very popular place to work because it served food. Applicants were always waiting in line for any available job. A major requirement was that anyone hired had to follow the rules of the club; the most important rule was not to steal. Employees were allowed to take leftovers during meal breaks, bread crusts cut from sandwiches, and other food if it was offered. But the temptation to take more than what was within the rule was a perpetual problem. It may seem harsh, but when limits are set, honesty requires employees to follow the rules or look somewhere else for a job. Honor requires honesty.

I well understood the hunger throughout Japan and probably didn't notice small food items that were obviously taken for family use. One night, however, the supervising duty cook caught the baker stealing a substantial amount of food, probably enough to sell on the black market, largely run by the yakuza, an organized gang similar to the mafia. I had no choice but to fire him. I later discovered that this man did belong to the yakuza and that someone in the mob was going to attack me and teach me a lesson.

At this time, I usually worked the night shift and transported the night employees to their homes. I then had to walk home on a lonely road. There were two routes to my home. One night, I sensed that somebody was waiting to ambush me on my normal route home, so I detoured and took the long way. Ogawa Sensei taught that avoiding danger was the spirit of kendo. Going out to look for trouble is an insult to the sword. After that, I changed to the day shift. One of the other employees tried to insult me by calling me a coward. I didn't really care that much about the insult. But then I was sure that the yakuza were taunting me so I would return to the night shift, where they would be waiting. I accepted their challenge.

I prepared myself mentally for a possible attack, but because I was unarmed, if they had a knife and stabbed me, I would probably be dead. However, I never gave the enemy any advantage in my thinking by assuming he was better or stronger than me. So I wasn't cautious or hesitant when I walked home in the dark, always remaining alert but calm. I wasn't afraid, having already decided I might die, and that was okay. One night I heard whispers, and all of a sudden, a man leaped in front of me with his knife raised above his head to strike. I moved to the side swiftly, just as I would have done if I were holding a sword. When you have practiced so much, you know the distance, you don't need the sword. When his momentum drove him past me, I turned to face him, and with a roaring *kiai* and fierce, unwavering stare, I rushed toward him. He turned and ran away, and I saw two other yakuza running with him. I continued to walk and arrived home safely.

Kendo spirit is part of the psyche of a man, just as the sword is an extension of the physical arm. Without a sword, I can still do kendo if I have kendo spirit. The word *seme* is defined as an attack, but more importantly it means "pressure." It can be visible or invisible, physical or mental, outer or inner, and ultimately it becomes part of the very being of a kendoist. Invisible *seme* is the most powerful. It can cause an opponent to seem hypnotized and retreat. My *seme* was not comparable to that of the legendary swordsmen like Yamaoka Tesshu (1836-1888), who was so powerful that he never had to use the sword. I had seen Ogawa Sensei win before the opponent even raised his sword, so powerful was his *seme*. But I do think it was kendo spirit that saved me that night although my opponents were not worthy enemies. A weapon, like a gun or a knife, is always a serious threat, however, and preferably avoided. That is the best strategy.

The next day, the head of the yakuza called me and invited me to join him at a party. Now I thought I really was dead. But I decided to go. Revenge would continue until it was satisfied, and the yakuza had a long memory. So, as we said in Hawaii, "Go for broke!" There is another saying, "If you don't go into the tiger's den, you won't get the cub." ("*Ko ketsu ni ira zumba koji wo ezu*"). If you can't avoid danger, and if you think it's necessary, put your life on the line and go for it. So I set my mind and body, accepted the invitation, and went to the party.

I walked in, and we both bowed. "I'm surprised you came," he said and called for sake.

"I came to die," I replied, "but if I'm going to die, I'll drink your sake first!"

"Ha!" he laughed. "So you have found the perfect place of existential freedom—don't give a damn! That is a most dangerous man."

We sat, and he poured sake. "I like you," he said, and laughed deeply. "Kampai!"

When his men reported their unsuccessful encounter with me, he thought maybe I was a kendoist. Now, he knew for sure. "You have a strong *hara*. I could use you." We both knew, of course, that it would not be possible for me to work for the yakuza. We drank more sake, then shochu, a powerful homemade distilled beverage. Kendo spirit had changed a bad situation to a good situation. But I drank too much. When I started to go home, refusing any help from his men, I took only one step from the second floor and landed in the koi pond across the hall. After that, I think his men carried me home.

Later, the two of us became good friends. He had great respect for kendo, but I don't think any of the members of the yakuza had formal kendo training. After the War, they ran much of the black market, but many thought of themselves as the West thinks of Robin Hood. They were conservative Japanese who did not accept the Occupation Forces. They believed food should be for the Japanese, not the Western military. They would steal food and other goods and give them to the people. The yakuza revered the old ways of the samurai and were angry when the Occupation Forces outlawed kendo and confiscated swords. Later, when carrying a gun was punished by a long jail sentence, waving swords became a favored way for the yakuza to intimidate their enemies. The yakuza leader could not comprehend what I thought I was protecting by working for the Occupation Forces. I was a kendoist, wasn't I, rooted in traditional Japan? Why help the Occupation? To steal from the enemy and kill them was acceptable, and if the goods were then distributed to the Japanese people, that was fine, too.

Taking from the rich and giving to the poor was a philosophy similar to the Communist Party line, but politically the two groups were almost directly opposite. The yakuza were considered right-wing nationalists, while the Japanese Communist Party (JCP) were thought to be left-wing threats. The Japanese Socialist Party (JSP) organized labor strikes; the yakuza helped to break strikes. All three organizations were tracked with keen interest by Occupation intelligence forces and the Japanese police, but the yakuza were not seriously pursued, especially since they broke up strikes and harassed the JSP and the JCP. The Cold War was in its formative stage, and the Communists were seen as the common enemy. I never had reason to betray my yakuza friend because the main focus of my intelligence activities concerned the JCP. Today things have changed. The yakuza is considered like the mafia and no longer compared to Robin Hood.

~

Empire Club employees in their uniforms. Mutsuko is in the middle of the back row.

Theft at the Empire Club included more than food. Employees

were also taking money. It was relatively easy as the currencies were confusing, and bookkeeping was sloppy. I watched carefully, and generally only reprimanded a person on the first offense. I tried to improve policies to correct internal management problems. That seemed the best solution instead of firing everybody. Because it seemed that everyone was a thief. Except one—Mutsuko Kawakami.

I watched Mutsuko, probably because she was pretty and didn't seem to like me. I was the boss, so many employees were friendly to me, perhaps hoping for special favors. Mutsuko was not like that. She did her job. She never took food. And even though she was a cashier and had many opportunities to steal money, she never took a yen. She was calm and never complained. At the end of the evening shift, I took all the lady employees home in the company car, a weapons' carrier truck. I would create a special route so I was sure to drop Mutsuko off last.

Maybe that was our courtship ritual. I don't know, but she eventually grew to like me, and, of course, I respected and really liked her. I took her home with me, and we were married with only her parents in attendance. Our wedding was entered into the family register. Our daughter Kazumi (Charlotte) was born in 1951. Now we had two daughters, the new baby and Miyuki, the daughter from my first marriage. From the beginning, the girls were raised as sisters.

During my last year in Kure, I was employed for a short time by the Atomic Bomb Casualty Commission (ABCC) as a dispatcher. From the bombings in 1945 to the First World Conference against Atomic and Hydrogen Bombs in 1955, the Occupation Forces repressed as much information as possible related to the atomic bomb. But political forces, if not the conservative Japanese government, would not let them forget Hiroshima and Nagasaki. Everything from medical problems among survivors, the need for reconstruction and government assistance programs, plans for conferences, both in Japan and internationally, all were perceived as a potential threat by the Americans. Both the JCP and the JSP were involved in the 1955 conference. Reorganization of labor and recruitment of new workers were major agendas. The JSP already had support from the General Council of Trade Unions of Japan. It was feared that the JCP would gain members because, from the beginning, they had denounced the Pacific War. Not only the defeat of Japan but especially the use of the atomic bomb strengthened their position. The JCP politically leaned toward China, and the JSP toward the Soviet Union. Both alliances were carefully monitored by the Occupation Forces.

~

While I was working for the Army Counter Intelligence Corps (CIC) in Kure, Captain Parker called, offering me a job at CIC in Matsue, the capital of Shimane Prefecture and about 250 miles from Kure. My reply was immediate. I quit my job in Kure and moved with my family to Matsue. I think it was late 1949. The Occupation Forces were now called the Security Forces.

In my new role in Matsue, I functioned as liaison between the Prefecture Police, the City Police, and the CIC. One day I noticed some kendo equipment at the Matsue City Hall. When I asked the police captain if we could play kendo, he replied that kendo was prohibited by the Occupation Forces. So then I asked the commanding officer at CIC if we could play kendo. Because he knew something about my background, he gave me permission. The police captain was surprised that permission was granted, but then he looked at me and grinned. A translator wanting to participate in sword practice? He thought it would be a big joke. His men could teach me a few things. But I saw them coming, and I was a little better with the sword. I beat them all, easily.

After that first practice, I sat on the sensei side instead of the student side and was recognized as a kendo man. I was welcome to practice with the police at any time. Kendo practice was part of me, a treasured part of my life that had been absent for too long. I hadn't realized it, but I was starved for practice. For me, kendo was as important as eating. With kendo, I found myself. I was alive again.

It had been more than three years since I had held a *shinai*. I hadn't thought much about it, but when I felt the sword in my hands, I realized how much I had missed kendo. There were many times at Busen that I would have been happy to skip practice. Now, it was hard for me to believe there had been times that I had ever been bored with practice. A whole year of *kirikaeshi*? When I was at Busen, I desperately wanted something new to work on, not just the same thing over and over. I was focused on my goals, on improving my skills, on winning tournaments, on being the best. But now, just holding a *shinai* in my hands and practicing felt great!

My translating job with the Counter Intelligence Corps expanded and became more exciting as well. I became a spy to a small degree. I identified several informers, listened to the information they provided about the JCP, and then reported to the CIC. My job was to find the facts: who participated, when and where meetings were held, and what was discussed. Captain Parker was especially interested in the gun trade. All the information I reported checked out to be correct. I accompanied the Matsue police and CIC when they went to parties, to interpret, of course, but also to keep my eyes and ears alert. This duty included trips to Tamatsukuri Onsen, a hot spring town near Matsue. I got to know the hot spring hotels and geishas quite well, activities that were usually restricted to the wealthy, but I had to be careful not to get too relaxed. I had to remain alert.

Gathering intelligence on a visit to Tamatsukuri Onsen, a hot spring resort.

My next assignment was more dangerous. One of the informants agreed to let me hide and listen to a meeting of the JCP planned to take place at his house. I hid in a small closet and heard firsthand all the plans for an upcoming demonstration.

I had to remain still, cramped, and hardly breathing, for a long time. Fortunately, I had learned how to do this at Busen. If I had been caught, I could have been killed.

That short stint was the end of my career as a spy. Captain Parker was transferred. Major Cassidy then hired me to continue to work for the CIC at Miho Air Force Base in the small town of Oshinozu, near Matsue, in the adjoining Tottori Prefecture. I was promoted to head translator/interpreter. My job was to instruct all the translators, who were mostly Japanese and couldn't interpret, and the interpreters, who did not know enough Japanese to converse freely with the Japanese.

With other translators and interpreters at Miho.
I am on the far right in the second row.

This new job gave me more time to associate with Major Cassidy, and I could still play kendo in the evenings. Housing was scarce so Dr. Kanno, who owned and operated a hospital in Matsue, arranged for me and my family to live in public housing in Matsue.

Our two daughters at the public housing in Matsue. Kazumi (Charlotte) is on the bicycle, and Miyuki (Norma) is standing behind her.

Commuting from Matsue to Miho Air Base was complicated. Every day I folded up my collapsible bicycle and boarded the train from Matsue Station to Yonago Station, then changed trains from Yonago to Oshinozu. Next I unfolded the bicycle and peddled to the Air Base. Coming home, I reversed the process.

While I was working at the Air Base, Dr. Kanno ran for

Matsue City Council, and I campaigned for him. After winning a seat on the City Council, he asked me to teach his sons English. I accepted, and so after work, I would stop by at his house and teach English to his two sons and another boy, who was a son of Dr. Kanno's friend, also a doctor.

After teaching the boys, I got to bathe in his nice big bathtub and enjoyed a great meal. The public housing where we lived did not have baths, so we had to use a public bath. In the summertime, Mutsuko and I bathed our daughters in an outside cement square tub. Of course, food was still scarce so whenever I ate at Dr. Kanno's, it meant more food for my wife and daughters.

While employed at Miho Air Base, I once again was lucky when a new opportunity was offered to me by AIU, American International Underwriters, an insurance company. I was acquainted with a Japanese secretary, a typist, who was rumored to be having an affair with the President of AIU, and she promoted my recruitment. I used my collapsible bicycle and rode around the base where Americans were living in Japanese houses. At first, it was very difficult trying to sell fire insurance to American officers. Sales were slow. I think it took about a month to sell the first policy—to a colonel who lived on the base. About a month later, his house burned to the ground. I helped the colonel's wife fill out the claim form. AIU reimbursed him so he didn't have to pay to replace the house and contents. News spread quickly that the fire insurance I sold covered everything in the home! All of a sudden, everyone on the base wanted fire insurance. During the daytime I worked for the CIC, but in my free time I sold more insurance than anybody in AIU. I made more money from selling insurance than the paycheck I got from the Japanese government for working at CIC. My wife was very happy!

Family Christmas celebration in Matsue, Japan. Front row: my younger daughter, Kazumi (Charlotte); my father, Shinichi; my elder daughter, Miyuki (Norma); my mother, Tameno; my sister-in-law, Fusako. Back row: my wife, Mutsuko (Mildred); me; my brother, Tomio (Brian).

Word also got around about my English teaching. The Governor of Shimane Prefecture sent for me. He wanted me to teach his daughter English in the evenings so she could help him learn how to buy American cars. The Japanese economy was recovering from the War, and demand for American products grew. When Occupation personnel returned to the States, their cars could be bought cheaply if the right connections were made. Not only the wealthy Japanese but also the police and city officials wanted cars. A new market was created—auto insurance. After an American officer wrecked his car in an accident, everyone wanted auto insurance, which I also sold. Major Cassidy told me to forget translation work. "Just sell insurance," he said, "and get rich like Americans!"

Major Cassidy and his family.

I was so successful at selling insurance that the secretary who had recommended me for the job took me to Tokyo to company headquarters. I received an award as a top seller for the company. After the ceremony, there was a big party with lots of food and drink. I had fun, drank sake, but did not fall into any fishponds.

I was getting rich, but I didn't know how to spend money. So long as my family had food and a house, money wasn't important to me. I just wanted to practice kendo as often as possible—after work, on weekends and holidays. At Busen, I usually practiced with higher ranked kendoists and lost many of the practice matches. Ogawa Sensei, of course, was unbeatable. He was the highest ranked kendoist in all of Japan, Tenth Dan! In Matsue, no one from the Matsue police or the Japanese Air Force (referred to as Defense Forces because the Occupation forbade Japan from having an offensive military) could beat me. But my winning streak in Matsue was about to change.

I was introduced to Ono Soichiro Sensei, whose dojo was in Tokyo. After the War he returned to his home in Matsue, where he had spent his youth. When he was in middle school, he was physically active in track and baseball as well as kendo. One day, Ashida Choichi Sensei, his kendo instructor, noted his potential and encouraged him to continue his practice. He became the captain of the Matsue High School kendo team. Ashida Sensei took him to Kyoto for the All Japan Kendo Taikai, where he was awarded Third Dan. It was unheard of for a high school student from a small country town to receive such a high rank.

At that time, his kendo sensei was Takano Sasaburo (1868--1950), one of the five people, along with Naito Sensei, who created the Nihon Kendo Kata during the early 1900s. He was the author of the book *Kendo* that included the *Gorin no Sho* (*The Book of Five Rings*) by Miyamoto Musashi that Miura Sensei had given me. Takano Sasaburo Sensei started Ono Sensei with the basics as if he were a beginner. He stressed the *kata* and the philosophy of Miyamoto Musashi.

During the years when I was at Busen and then, after the War, Ono Sensei and Ogawa Sensei were titans, the reigning pillars in kendo. Ono Sensei was Tokyo; Ogawa Sensei was Kyoto. Ono Sensei was Eighth Dan and in his fifties; Ogawa Sensei was Tenth Dan and in his seventies. Both were large men, Ono Sensei being slightly shorter than Ogawa Sensei, who was more than six feet tall. They met only once as far as I know. That was when I was in Matsue in 1954 at the Sixth Annual Championship tournament between Shimane and Tottori Prefectures.

Kendo tournament between Shimane and Tottori Prefectures, 1954.

Ogawa Sensei was there as a dignitary, but Ono Sensei participated with the other kendoists although he didn't compete. He beat everyone. Also participating were three graduates from Busen: Onishi Tomoji Sensei (class of 1939), who owned a stationery store in Matsue; Furuse Joh Sensei (class of 1931), who was a school principal; and Kawakami Tokuzo from Taisha (class of 1930). They were the toughest. I couldn't beat them, nor could any of the other competitors.

But Ono Sensei was magic! At our first match, I couldn't get near him. It was as if he had some powerful inner quality and knew everything I would do before I did it. I felt as if his pressure (*seme*) was so powerful that I couldn't move.

Seme creates a relationship. I felt Ono Sensei's calm and compassion as well as his awesome power, the invisible fire that boils within. I knew he was all about spirit and perception, not judgment. I never felt like he was criticizing me. I knew I was the most fortunate man in the world to encounter such a great soul.

After that first practice, when I froze, I discovered that I could move again, or maybe he allowed me to move. He was kind and practiced with me. After practice, I'd take him out for sake and sushi. Now I knew what to do with my money. There was enough insurance money so we could indulge ourselves. We would talk kendo stories and kendo philosophy for hours. I would ask questions and then listen. Observe and listen. Practice and think about what was said. These are the thoughts of Musashi. Now I started to put them into practice.

Ono Sensei was always positive. There are no problems. Challenges are not difficulties but opportunities. If they are huge, all the better. The bigger the challenge, the greater the opportunity. Work harder. "The Ten Commandments are don'ts," he noted. "Make them positive. 'Be honest,' rather than 'don't steal'; 'be generous, make life' rather than 'do not kill.'" His examples were numerous. Kendo talk became life talk. And Ono Sensei applied it to everything.

To Ono Sensei, the sword is to make life, *Katsu Jin Ken*, not to take life. By the end of the Meiji period, the sword of the samurai used for battle had evolved into the Way of the Sword. The old battle legends remained popular as part of Japanese lore, but if there were any doubts, the Pacific War pounded home the lesson that the old ways of violence and death had to change. The sword is useless against guns and bombs dropped from airplanes. The wars of the samurai are not the wars of the twentieth century. The misuse of the sword leads to despicable acts that dishonor the spirit of the sword. Violence is not the Way. The purpose of the sword is to create a human being, to forge and temper the spirit. The world is not certain; all that is certain is what is within you.

Despite all that had happened during the War, Ono Sensei said, "Have no regrets. Regret is the painful recognition of what is compared unfavorably with what might have been or should have been. Now is all we have. It is where we live. The sword teaches you to be present in each moment."

He also stressed meditation. That, too, focuses on the present moment. If the mind is consumed by regret for the past or worry about the future, it is full and has no room for the present. If the mind is full, nothing can be added. Before kendo practice, there are a few minutes of meditation to become present to practice, to empty all other thoughts but what is happening in the dojo. But Ono Sensei stressed the importance of longer meditation, morning and evening. "Meditation is the most powerful motion," he reiterated, "and the most difficult."

He won all tournaments, but he never stressed winning. He talked instead of the matches that were close calls, strange twists and turns of fate, unpredictable finishes. Sometimes this would lead to discussions of particular skills, but he never spoke of practicing a skill explicitly as a goal for winning. With practice, a skill was not something you attained, but something you became. Kendo was joyous for him in the way that music was joyous. He played the shakuhachi, and his wife played the shamisen. They practiced together, harmonized and complemented each other. Their musical duets were like the kendo *kata*, with parts alternating within the same song as one would take the lead and then the other, improvising as they continued to practice. Theirs was a marriage of spirits. He believed that his breath remained stronger than that of most kendoists because of playing the shakuhachi. At Ninth Dan, he was active in kendo until his mid-nineties, when he died, several weeks after a kendo tournament he attended in Kyushu. His wife, also in her nineties, continued to play the shamisen.

Ono Sensei saw adaptation as a natural part of evolution, just as kendo had to evolve. "No regrets. Have a positive attitude and do what is most beneficial for the people of Japan." It was said that Japan "embraced defeat" after the War, but Ono Sensei compared this to the relationship built in kendo. "To win, you must be one with your opponent, but this takes years of practice." Acceptance of defeat restored life to Japan, and by 1964 Japan could boast the strongest economy in Asia. The Japanese attitude was the spirit that made life, the spirit rooted in the Way of the Sword. War is simple. Peace is complex.

In the late 1950s, my life changed too and became complicated. My first wife's brother was relentless in searching for me, and he discovered where I was living. To avoid danger to my family, we had to move, and I had to change jobs. My brother, Tomio, worked for the Sharp Company, a ships' supplier. Through that company, I was hired as a seaman on the *USS Universe Admiral*, a tanker that carried crude oil from Kuwait to Idemitsu Refinery in Tokuyama. Each trip took a month—two weeks to get to Kuwait, one day to fill the tanker, and two weeks to return to Tokuyama. The heat was excruciating. With this job, I had only one day a month with my family and no days for kendo.

Posing with one of my shipmates on the *USS Universe Admiral.*

This was unbearable but, again, I was lucky. My younger sister, Jean Kessel, sponsored my family to emigrate to the United States. My brother found us cheap passage on the *Oregon Mail*, a merchant ship. I had spent twenty-one years in Japan, and on New Year's Day, 1960, my wife, daughters, and I landed in Tacoma, Washington. My sister welcomed us to the United States. Our new life in America had begun.

5
Void
空

To start with, killing is not the Way of mankind. Killing is the same for people who know about fighting and for those who do not.

—Miyamoto Musashi

In 1985, my wife, Mildred (Mutsuko), was diagnosed with biliary cirrhosis, a type of cirrhosis not associated with alcohol consumption. The doctors gave her only two years to live unless she had a liver transplant. But she refused, saying, "Don't be silly. I am old! Give the liver to a younger person." That was the kind of person she was. She died on April 5, 1990.

As she grew weaker, I took care of her at home, and she lived for five years, much longer than the doctors had predicted. Because she had been sick for so long, I thought I was prepared for her death. But only in my mind was I prepared, and that is not enough. I had no words to express . . . Even now. My small portion of the world was the same. The streets of Tacoma, where we had been living since 1966, were no different Everything was exactly the same. But to me, everything was different. There was only this, an empty place I'd never dreamed of and would never have chosen.

In the days after her death, there was much to do, but it was all a blur. The funeral announcement for the newspaper, making arrangements for cremation, the funeral service at the Tacoma Buddhist Temple, hospital equipment to be returned, unused prescriptions to be thrown away, responding to many condolences from friends, even canceling my wife's *Fujin no Tomo* subscription, the monthly magazine published by the Japanese women's Christian organization she had belonged to for many years. Our daughters, Norma and Charlotte, helped to sort clothes and jewelry and printed a good picture of Mildred for our Buddhist altar, the *butsudan*.

Our *butsudan*. I put Mildred's picture there after her passing.

I opened the *butsudan* every morning, lit the candles and incense, and chanted the Shoshinge. I felt the physical objects in the *butsudan* carried something of the essence of Mutsuko. While performing this ritual, I felt the presence of her spirit.

But after that morning ritual, there was just me, alone, in the house on Verde Street, the house that Mildred had chosen to buy so many years ago. I kept one double bed and a chest of drawers in each bedroom. For efficiency, I moved the beds to the center of the rooms so it would be easier to make them. In the living room, I left one couch and one table. I closed the drapes. These were things I could control, and at night, weak and uncertain, lacking energy, I fell into a dreamless sleep—sleep, a means of transport, of escape. But there is never really escape. There is only one choice—life.

Routine offers consolation. Habit demands action, but because it is well known, it also allows relaxation. It can prepare us for what is to come. There is enormous freedom achieved by paying attention to tiny details. In the weeks and months after Mildred died, every morning I performed the same routine. I would run two miles, do *suburi* (a kendo exercise), and then clean and cook and pay the bills as Mildred had instructed. But it was not enough.

My spirit was weak. I guess you could say that I was free, ready to blow in the wind, but this freedom seemed more like an anchor. I felt like a stone. Moreover, this was not true freedom because I was attached to the illusion of "not caring." So I filled the immense, fearful, empty times of dread and a yearning I could barely define by becoming more active in the Tacoma Buddhist Temple, where Mildred had found such satisfaction.

I studied, chanted, meditated, and taped Buddhist texts to my wall and breakfast table. These were reminders of how to fill a hunger that is the very claim of life, and gradually they started a train of events that set into motion one small point of convention—the *Michi*, the Way—that became the sustenance for the rest my life.

When Mildred was terminally ill, I quit my job and even quit kendo to take care of her. But with a year for mourning passed after her death, my kendo friends began to visit, encouraging me to be the sensei for the Tacoma Kendo Club, to participate in the Seattle Kendo Club, and to teach kendo at Tacoma Community College. I told my friends that I was not good anymore now that I was in my mid-seventies, as if I had even been "good" before. But they finally persuaded me that it was time to do kendo again, to experience the present, and prepare for the future. They convinced me I had a responsibility to carry as much as possible from the past traditions into the twenty-first century. Once again, kendo created life in me.

~

Ogawa Sensei, my teacher at Busen, often reminded me that *seppuku* (ritual suicide) was no longer the Way. Instead, one should "live to serve!" After Mildred died, life seemed to have turned colorless, but I would live to give and be useful, to serve the community unselfishly for the rest of the days remaining to me. Yes, for the *Michi*—the Way—but that is presumptuous of me to say. I am not great like Naito Takaharu Sensei, who left Tokyo, inspired by the weight of the telegram which said, "Come for the sake of the *Michi*" to create the first martial arts school in Japan, Budo Senmon Gak'ko (Busen), in Kyoto.

Unlike Naito Sensei, I'm a nobody! So I remind myself, "I'm not teaching kendo. All I'm doing is sharing what I have learned from my former senseis. I am sensei only in the literal translation: *sen* means "born ahead." And I am now, at eighty-seven, almost the oldest practicing kendoist in the Pacific Northwest.

My decision to return to kendo reflected the concept of filial piety. My father would have wanted me to continue. And I was carrying the lineage of Miura Kenji Sensei and his senseis as well as Ogawa Kennosuke Sensei and his senseis. Moreover, after Mildred's death, I had had time to reflect, to study Buddhism, to do as Musashi advised and meditate on the "strategy" so I could try to consciously apply the lessons to my own life.

During the pre-War days, Nakamura Tokichi Sensei founded the Hokubei Butokukai (North American Martial Virtue Association) in 1929. The movement had overwhelming support from the Isseis, who were starving for the Japanese spirit, as a way to create life in the Nisei youth along the Pacific Coast from Washington to California. The Tacoma Kendo Club was formed in 1940. Some thought that by learning kendo, these young Nisei would become an asset to Japan; others hoped kendo would help to improve US-Japanese relations and improve the morality of the young kendoists.

After Pearl Harbor, the US government became suspicious of the kendo clubs. The FBI investigated the Butokukai in 1942 and arrested many members and organizational leaders. The government banned all Japanese-Americans from owning firearms or swords—even the bamboo *shinais* used in kendo. After the war, many Japanese-Americans didn't realize that they could start to practice kendo again.

When I came to Tacoma in 1966, I became active in sharing kendo with others. Initially, I taught kendo to Boy Scouts in the Tacoma Buddhist Temple basement. Later I was the founding Charter President of the Washington State Kendo Federation, now known as the Pacific Northwest Kendo Federation, and also one of the founding members of the University of Washington Kendo Club. For many years, I enjoyed teaching kendo throughout the Northwest.

Now that I am eighty-seven years old, I have discovered that old age completes our form. My face is wrinkled and shows my age. Paradoxically, this is also the face with which I was born—

wrinkled, toothless, with wisps of hair. Today I am nearly deaf, my eyes weakening so that I have to use a magnifying glass to read standard-size print, and I can no longer drive a car. But I can still see the light and feel the sun. *Kan Mu Sho Kyu* means, "May the Bu, or Mu (god of martial arts), shed light eternally on everyone." This is not about religion but about nature, something greater than all of us. The *Do*. The Way. No matter how old I am, the light brings energy and vitality, so while the light remains and the invisible wind carries me, I can act. I can live now. This is how the sword has made life in me, to create a relationship with myself, with my heart (*kokoro*), to create a relationship whole-heartedly with plants and animals and other human beings. This is what *Katsu Jin Ken* means to me.

When I started kendo, I used to say to myself that I "wish" I could win, I "like" to win. Then I would say I "want" to win, I "need" to win. Then I "must" win. Now I don't *need* to win. I *am* winning and appreciating every day of my life. I am a very fortunate elder.

One of my friends from Tacoma or Seattle kendo always offers to drive me to practice. We have kendo talk along the way. And when I get to the dojo, I play kendo dummy. The students line up, and I *keiko* with everyone, including the children. I am the receiver and give them openings to strike: "Can you hit me? Try it. Come on, come on. Get me!" So my *teki* (opponent) receives the feeling of winning but also the mysterious toughness of receiving without being bruised. But if a more advanced *teki* is overconfident or misses the opening, I redirect the strike and turn it back on him. Then the *teki* learns that his technique is not as well understood as he thought. He is encouraged to practice more and also given a reminder about humility. When I play kendo dummy, I'm just trying to help the other guy improve.

One of the most useful skills I learned as a schoolboy in Wahiawa was typing. After the War, of all things, I was treasured as a typist. Typing bought rice. But typing has evolved to become keyboarding, or typing on the computer. Kendo attitude requires adapting to change. My computer is a great gift. I can e-mail relatives and kendo friends all over the world, often attaching pictures. Fortunately, because of my deafness, I don't have to hear well and depend on the telephone. I just key in my message and send and receive in Nihongo (Japanese) or English.

Just this June I received an e-mail from New York City from Atsushi Horiike, who is the husband of Miyuki, Ogawa Kinnosuke Sensei's great-granddaughter. He had read a small article about me in the November 2004 issue of *Kendo Nippon Magazine.* He discovered that at Kodokan, the dojo where I had studied in Kyoto, I babysat for Ogawa Sensei's granddaughter

Michiko-san, who is his wife's aunt. Through e-mail, he was able to contact me, and once again across all these years, I am communicating with the family of Ogawa Sensei. Kodokan is gone. But the relationships created by kendo never end, and now the evolution of modern technology allows those relationships to make me alive. I am not a lonely elder.

I receive e-mails from senseis all across the United States—from Chicago and North Carolina and Hawaii. Sometimes they ask questions. I answer as best I can. Ogushi Sensei e-mails me from Tokyo and has even visited me. Peter Mizuki, who is on the faculty at the Nippon Daigaiku, came to see me. David Pan returned to Taiwan after receiving his medical degree, but he still visits Tacoma, and he arranged for me to travel to Taiwan so that I could visit him and *keiko* with his senseis. What a privilege to be able to travel and contribute as well as to be entertained. I especially enjoy the parties, where sake is served.

Current kendo students also e-mail me. I can reply to their questions at my leisure and add more detail than would be possible in a spoken conversation since I am effectively deaf. Because I have more time to think about what I want to say, I can customize my answers so they will be relevant to their lives and professions.

Even those who practiced kendo only briefly, sometimes long ago, have contacted me. Like the swordsmiths of samurai days, who pounded and polished until the strength of their blades matched the strength of their will, a kendo friend who practices carpentry understands that he must be skilled and unhesitating when he cuts a board, recalling the lessons of Miyamoto Musashi to guide his craft.

A fiddler friend practiced kendo twenty years ago for several years. He injured his back and can no longer do kendo, but he now enjoys samurai movies. Remembering what I had said about Miyamoto Musashi, he e-mailed me with a question related to his violin playing. He told me that he practices his violin faithfully but is dissatisfied with his performance. I encouraged him to apply kendo attitude to his violin playing. As a result, he is no longer inhibited by his ego, which caused him to fear that he would not be good enough. Now he does the very best he can, and his performing is from the heart. He learned that showing to share is not the same as showing off. It is as easy and graceful as friendship. Practicing the violin makes life in him and gives him a glimpse of the best in himself, which he gives without reservation to others. That is *Katsu Jin Ken*. I think that perhaps his attitude toward fiddle practice and sharing music is similar to that of Ono Sensei, who practiced the shakuhachi flute as well as the sword until the day he died.

Kendo attitude has also helped Daniel Ichinaga, an attorney in Seattle who practices at Seattle Kendo. Not only is he Third Dan, but he also listens with his *hara*, not just his intellect, and applies the attitude of kendo to all aspects of his life. He practices law; he practices kendo. It is the same. There is a vector, but no end, a direction without a fixed destination. Lawyers practice their entire lives to shape and hone their skills to serve their clients' best interests with elegant simplicity. The well-seasoned attorney is not distracted in court. In a court fight or preparing for trial, a lawyer is sensitive to whether the other side is setting the pace or applying the pressure. Each wants this control, but whoever creates the relationship assumes control. If the opposing attorney tries to provoke anger to force a response, he will gain control. If his pressure is met without an emotional response, he will become frustrated and lose control. This is the challenge of a court fight. Like kendo, no emotion. Reading the intentions of others, taking control of the courtroom becomes second nature—but only after years of practice and experience.

Seemingly, there is a world of difference between Daniel Ichinaga and Zeke, but both have developed kendo attitude.

I met Zeke when I was working at McNeil Island Federal Penitentiary in the mid-1980s. In this job, I supervised the inmates in their work assignments. Unlike some of the other employees, who treated the inmates badly, I brought my kendo philosophy with me to this work. Every morning I would lead the inmates in kendo exercises. Zeke was one of these inmates. He was sincerely interested in kendo and listened to *The Book of Five Rings* on audiotape. But because he was imprisoned, he could not practice kendo in a dojo. Like Miyamoto Musashi, he taught himself and practiced with wooden swords and cardboard tubes. The more he practiced, the more he understood about the spirit of Musashi. To him, this was a gift.

In 1985, when Mildred became ill, I left the job at the penitentiary to care for her. Later, Zeke wrote to me saying he would like to show me what he had learned, even though it was not traditional. "Someday I will stand before you in the outside world, and we can play kendo. Standing before you will not only be myself, but also my senseis—you and Miyamoto Musashi."

In 1997, when he had been released from prison, we did meet, talked, and continued to communicate by e-mail. He had many challenges including a strenuous job driving a truck and constant worry about his four-year-old granddaughter, who was living in a drug house. It would have been easy for him to take the easy way and give up. That is when the true *Katsu Jin Ken* comes out. We must live through these difficult times with confidence and strength of will and have the guts to realize that these are challenges; they will pass, and instead of failure, we will have success. The situation with his granddaughter was controlling him until he took the offensive. He wrote, "I realized I had died long ago. What I'm living now is an extra bonus. Maybe this was my purpose for living so long through so much." With a calm mind and resolute intent, knowing well that his actions could have returned him to prison or even resulted in his death, he walked into the drug house and met no resistance. His battle was to create life for his family. He is now living with the child and her grandmother. He is working energetically without distraction for his family. This is the *Katsu Jin Ken* attitude that makes life in him. I feel proud to know Zeke, who is the bravest of all and a genuine student of Miyamoto Musashi.

~

Because I am in the sunset of my life, it is befitting that I respond not only to younger kendo friends but to others who are growing old. I talk more now than when I was younger. Maybe that is one of the compensations of age; it doesn't require strong muscles to talk. I probably talk too much and become repetitive. But whatever I say or do must feel true to me and be of benefit to the listener.

I shared kendo with a group of senior citizens in 1995. I try to be a frame, sharing what I've learned, which they can fill according to their abilities. It was fun. We did the Japanese aerobic radio exercises and some kendo exercises. I even did *kata* (ritualized kendo movement) with them, but I did not recommend daily kendo practice. It is not impossible to begin *suburi* (strenuous kendo exercises) when you are old, but it is not very realistic. When practicing kendo, you have to consider your present circumstances, not dream about something that is far away or unattainable.

Kendo attitude is very practical. For instance, once I was in my eighties, I became a "kendo driver." Practicing kendo taught me to always be aware of what was around me when I was driving. Watch three cars behind, three ahead, and observe what is happening to the right and the left. Good day, bad day—no difference. There is no place for emotion, just awareness of each moment so that you can make your movements and communicate them decisively to other drivers. With this attitude, the elderly can be good drivers. But when my hearing failed, not even kendo driving was possible. One day I barely avoided an accident because I entered an intersection deaf to the siren of a fire truck screaming through the red light. After that incident, I knew I had to stop driving because I would endanger others. Realizing one's limitations, that, too, is kendo attitude.

It was really kendo attitude we were sharing in that class of senior citizens—a reminder not just to merely sweat with exercise but also to become conscious of our instincts. We breathe, we see, and we walk, all unconsciously. After kendo, we breathe, we see, and we walk consciously, with appreciation. I shared a saying with them: "I'm right now at my youngest. In an hour I'll be an hour older. Tomorrow my body and my mind will be one day older. So I'll do my very best, right NOW!" This is living in the "present moment." You can't hear, except now. You can't see, except now. You can't touch, except now. This is a positive attitude. *Katsu Jin Ken* is relevant. It demands living in the present moment.

Living in the moment, one implicitly realizes the reality of death. It is easy to deny death. Violence and death, even war, have become prime-time television entertainment. Yet avoiding any thoughts of one's own death is particularly easy for young people and part of their natural exuberance for life.

But the frailties and illnesses suffered by the old are strong reminders of our mortality. We are born, we age, we become sick, we die. But, in our consumer society, this process of human life becomes a source of profit for others. Your trouble is my profit. Your pain is my profit. Your enjoyment is my profit. Your safety is my profit. So television commercials tell us what to buy to fix ourselves. Modern medicine is supposed to cure us, and products and procedures offer ways to keep our appearance and bodies from showing our age. The elderly are especially vulnerable to these commercials.

Five hundred years ago the *Yojo Kun*, a classical Japanese text authored by samurai physician Kaibara Ekiken, listed other ways to take care of our bodies. Basically, it advised us to keep the body tuned by exercise, fueled by good food, rested with naps, and shined with positive attitude. This is still good advice.

We are human beings. We don't want to die. We'll never be ready to die. But fear is worse than death. Death is just the end of life. That is a given. What you know can be endured. But even more important, every moment becomes more precious. I don't disapprove of doctors, and I have a yearly physical. I had high blood pressure, typical for the elderly, and I was prescribed pills, but until about a decade ago, I controlled my blood pressure by eating a low-salt diet. Then I installed a hot tub in my house and soaked every morning after my exercises and every evening before going to sleep. I discovered that soaking is also a good time to watch television. It is very pleasant, reduces my blood pressure, and helps my arthritis. I no longer take pills for high blood pressure or to hide the pain from my old joints. Take care of your body! No one else can. Ignore the television commercials that are talking to you, scaring you, and telling you to buy, always to buy.

A healthy body helps to create a healthy attitude and vice versa. But just as I can guide but cannot teach anyone kendo, I cannot make anyone healthy. You have to do that for yourself. It's your choice. My choice is to practice kendo, practice health, practice positive attitude. I also practice sharing because it is an antidote for self-pity, which selfishly admits no needs but its own and results in the hopeless grievances of disappointments, mistakes and criticism.

I love winners! But a winner is not necessarily a champion with a perfect, healthy body or someone who is rich in the eyes of the world. A winner is someone who always does his or her best, contributes to others, and recognizes that a simple life can also be a good life. If I am poor, it's okay. If I am rich, that's okay too. A winner is someone who applies himself or herself with diligence to solve one problem after another.

In 1997, after fifty years of absence, I returned to Kyoto for the 93rd Kendo Taikai, an annual event where experienced practitioners gather to play kendo and socialize. I was a seventy-eight-year-old man with a Seventh Dan Kyoshi and a drive to go for Eighth Dan. I honed my three *shinais* so that they were in perfect condition, checked my outfit very closely, and even ironed my *hakama*. I was an elderly man just as excited as a kid with a new toy. However, when I faced my classmates, I knew my skill level was inferior. The difference was that they practiced every day with higher rankers, including Ninth Dan Hanshi. Not only did I not practice every day, but I served as a kendo dummy, playing with lower rankers. Needless to say, I didn't get my Eighth Dan. So I guess some would say I was not a winner. But I had a wonderful time playing kendo for a week, drinking sake, and catching up with my classmates. I was greatly challenged and learned more about kendo. I did my best. Talking with my classmates also made me realize that I am one of the fortunate ones. Many had died. Most were not healthy enough to continue their kendo. I felt very fortunate. I can still play kendo!

Life is really very simple. Four things: we get up, eat, move, and then sleep. Pay attention to it all. Eat well; rest your body. How we fill our moments of moving is our choice. There are realistic choices we can make to adjust to our older bodies and prepare ourselves so we will not become a burden to others. We can write our wills, give instructions for our funerals, tell our children our history so they will know about our lives. Prepare practically. A simple routine, such as exercise each morning, creates a structure and a purpose, a practice that is also healthy. Stick with it. But continue to be alive.

A life seems to hold much more substance when it has been deliberate and purposeful rather than scattered. It anchors you, especially in old age, when everything begins to fade away. *Mitsugo no tamashii hyaku made* is an old saying that means what is created in you by age three will last for a hundred years. I was lucky. I was guided to kendo early in life, and despite challenges, I have stuck with it. For me, kendo is the *Michi*. Kendo is the Sword that has made my life. Kendo is *Katsu Jin Ken*.

So I say, "I've practiced to die. I'm prepared to die. I'm ready to die. But I'm not dead yet! And I'm going to continue on as if there is no end, enjoying every precious moment of my life.

6
My Kendo Philosophy
私の剣道哲学

One thousand days of keiko
begins the forging and tempering.
Ten thousand days of keiko
begins to polish what I have forged and tempered.

—Miyamoto Musashi

DAYS, THE WHOLE DAY, NOT a couple of hours a day. Miyamoto Musashi uses numbers to illustrate how much time is needed to acquire the state of being comfortable and confident, to become polished so there is no struggle or need to remember to do a certain thing to acquire another level. The Way is long. The Way is never ending. But it calls to some of us. And leads us to the sword or the bow or the tea ceremony, to that which makes life in us.

Developing kendo wisdom takes more than a lifetime. During my long life, I have read and reread *The Book of Five Rings* by Musashi, both in the currently popular English translation as well as the original old Japanese edition included in *Kendo*, a comprehensive book written more than a hundred years ago by Takano Sasaburo Sensei. This was the book that Miura Sensei gave me in 1938, when I left Hawaii to study at Busen in Japan. I also studied Satsuo Chuzo Sensei's book *Kendo No Manabi Kata*

(*How to Learn Kendo*) in both Japanese and English translation. I watched kendo movies and videos and read magazine articles in both Japanese and English. I continue to study to this day, although less as my eyes are no longer as strong as they once were. I can't count the number of times I've read *The Book of Five Rings*. All true kendo senseis are students of Miyamoto Musashi.

Since 1994, when I started to think about writing my autobiography, I began to share my thoughts with Tanaka Chichi Sensei, my sensei at Seiho Chugak'ko, the high school I attended in Japan, and also with my senseis from Busen, including Tsuzaki Kenkei Sensei (my freshman year sensei) and Sato Chuzo Sensei (my sophomore year sensei).

I not only respect the past, but I continue to try to understand—stand under—the timeless wisdom of the past. A Buddhist chant, the Amida Kyo, starts off with *Nyoze Gamon*, which means, "Thus I have heard." Physically, philosophically, and culturally, all the lessons I've learned from my physical senseis and my spiritual senseis from the past live in my heart today and forever.

Each time I read *The Book of Five Rings*, my feeling that the sword is to create life (*Katsu Jin Ken*) becomes stronger. The roots of kendo go back to the development of the Japanese sword in the days of the samurai, when the sword was used in warfare. During the peaceful Edo period (1603-1867), kendo evolved, and the armor and bamboo sword (*shinai*) were introduced to make it safer. In the late nineteenth century, the modern form of kendo was established. It combined various styles from across Japan and became part of the formal education system in the schools.

As kendo is practiced today, no one gets killed, but it is still warfare. Now the war is to create a better person. Certainly, the All Japan Kendo Federation, Zen Nippon Kendo Renmei (founded in 1952), commonly called Zen Ken Ren, espouses that the objective of kendo is The Way (*Do*) to create a decent human being through the study of the sword. This is The Path. From all my experience and my study, I have come to my own way of thinking: kendo is warfare—war with the self to improve the self.

~

I am often asked how I can use the sword to create a good human being out of my student. In a sense, I am being asked how I teach philosophy. My answer is simple: "I can't!" The operative word in the question is "teach." No one can teach kendo philosophy because teaching is about knowledge. So the focus of the question must be reframed: How can we practice so that the students themselves will choose this Way to forge and temper their spirit into kendo spirit. All I can do is guide the practice and throw out words like sowing seeds. So I begin practice by throwing out just a few words: "Why do we do kendo?" I don't expect a dialogue. Maybe the seeds will take root, maybe not. The only thing I can tell my students, right up front, the first day, is that kendo is not for self-defense. "Tell" time is done. Now it is "show" time.

The only restriction in kendo classes is that the student must want to learn kendo. However, children less than six years old are perhaps too young. A mother once asked me if her son could take kendo. I replied that I did not accept a student unless that student, not his mother, wanted to learn. I know that young people, especially, come for the sport. Like all sports, there is competition, a winner and a loser, judges and referees, rules and regulations, fouls and penalties, trophies and award celebrations, and very unique uniforms and equipment.

I welcome whoever comes, but I don't pursue those who do not stay. If the kids come for the sport, that is what they will get. If adults come to master a powerful weapon, that is what they will get, at least until they realize that a sword is neither a realistic nor effective weapon for the twenty-first century. Expectations limit possibilities. With time, maybe a student's expectations will evolve. Or not. If he or she is merely curious or looking for quick diversion, they will move on to something else.

At the beginning of a new class, I share my own experiences. I am just part of the pipeline, a messenger who guides them through the physical skills, the craft, and helps them become familiar with the equipment and the types of swords. It is natural that beginning students are frustrated with physical issues, with their awkwardness. We practice the techniques (*waza*) including *suburi* (exercises) and footwork and compete with each other. *Keiko* (practice) is kendo playing. It can be fun.

When I started to learn kendo, I was not thinking about *Do*. Certainly, I was not thinking of death. Those attitudes evolve over years. I was thinking about fun and anticipating ice cream after practice. When I developed skills, I was thinking of winning competitions. With enough practice, the physical body knowledge begins to evaporate; it becomes a part of your skill. Then you can really win competitions. I suppose that I was attached to the egotism of success. So really, in that sense, there is not much difference between kendo seventy-five years ago and kendo today.

Right from the beginning, there are rituals that are different from those of most other sports—*reigi*, the etiquette and traditions of kendo. However, tradition just for its own sake is empty unless it leads to a deeper truth. The *Do* (The Way) starts with the first ritual bow, which conveys courtesy and respect. The values of *Do* are not hidden. They are present and discernible on the surface in all training activities, but students are not necessarily able to recognize them. *Do* is not "tell" but "show." It is with *reigi*, the sensei, and the senior practitioners that the unstated initiation into the *Do* begins.

The sensei or senior instructor is one key to transmitting the legacy and validating core values. He sets the standard. That is why I say this is an awesome responsibility. But one shouldn't take oneself too seriously. Self-importance is attachment to ego. Thus, a sensei is more than someone who has earned a high rank and won tournaments or, as in some other sports, made millions of dollars. A kendo sensei must not be leading kendo classes for money. Wealth is not a value of *Do*, so getting rich cannot be a motivation for students to emulate. But the sensei is more than just a role model. I cannot create a good kendoist, but by my practice I create myself and perhaps inspire a student to practice to create kendo in himself. Therefore, the sensei's bearing and character are the nonverbal living example of the teachings. In the olden days, that was enough. The sensei treated students correctly but often with neither warmth nor verbal encouragement.

But today, in our multicultural society, that is not enough. The sensei must show the relationship to whatever is being taught within the context of life. Therefore, I begin at a very mundane level. I explain what the various parts of the dojo are and what they mean. It doesn't take much time.

More importantly, I will, initially at least, sweep the dojo. And if I don't, new students will see that senior rankers are doing so. Students rarely have the privilege of cleaning the dojo on their first day. The dojo is not like a gym, where you play basketball after the janitor has cleaned it. Cleaning the dojo before beginning practice is considered an honor. This is not merely janitorial work. It is spiritual training, an act that ritually cleanses the spirit, the *hara*. It is intended to purify your soul so the practice that follows will be pure and sincere.

The dojo is a place of great violence and great serenity. Thus, it is a place of tremendous authority and abject humility. It requires the same kind of respect and discipline as is used when making a samurai sword. When the sword is being tempered and forged, the anvil must be clean. With kendo, the dojo is the anvil, and the steel to make the sword is the student. The instructor is the hammer. The reason for sweeping the dojo isn't just because the dojo is dirty. Often the dojo doesn't actually need cleaning. But even after seventy-five years of practicing kendo, sweeping the dojo reminds me to be humble and to respect the place that has allowed me to polish myself to create life in me. At Kodokan and Busen, it also taught me to endure hardship.

Sometimes in American universities, it is difficult to distinguish the teacher from the student. Often the students will even address the teacher by his or her first name. The traditional hierarchy of the martial arts does not allow this type of informality, although the consistent use of the term "sensei," both in and out of the dojo, is losing favor.

There is an old kendo saying that there are only two rules to remember. First, do as Sensei says. And second, when in doubt, refer to Rule One. Today, this does not mean blind obedience to the sensei but rather respect for seniority that has been earned through experience, tradition, and proper conduct. Hierarchy also establishes the relationship required for leading those with less experience. Seniority is balanced by obligation.

Respect does not just travel up the line. Everyone is respected despite their differences. I am dedicated to you as you are dedicated to me because we both respect and are dedicated to kendo. In kendo, there are not separate classes for beginners and those with more experience or for students of different ages or genders. Because of this inclusiveness, the dojo becomes a strong community, with students helping, encouraging, and depending on one another. The focus within the community is on each individual's development. Because of these individual differences, especially between children and adults, no negativity or demeaning criticism is allowed. Only encouragement—always encouragement.

In describing the atmosphere within the dojo, I use the analogy of a rock tumbler. Rocks that are collected may be dull and rough around the edges, but they have great potential for beauty. They are thrown together, both little rocks and bigger rocks, into a tumbler filled with water and bounced against each other as they are constantly turned. They clatter and bang through the process noisily. And what is the result? Smooth and shiny polished rocks that have become, in many instances, beautiful pieces of art. So it is with kendo students. I polish you as you polish me. No one is teaching another, but all are just bumbling about together. Not everyone will train long enough in the dojo to become a work of art, but all will be changed. I remember a Zen saying that goes something like this: "Like the pebbles in a bag, the monks polish one another."

Respect for the sensei and the dojo and all the learners is the first lesson of discipline in kendo. How do you learn to respect yourself if you have no respect for others or for what you are doing? Bowing is a form of respect, as is attentive, quiet listening. Discipline does not mean punishment. External discipline is based on control and fear. But kendo discipline is restricted according to rituals that are engrained in this rich tradition. Sometimes these rituals are misunderstood as mere ceremonies. Perhaps a better way to think of them is as a way to help focus ourselves, a way to return to the center. Sweeping the dojo is really cleansing ourselves to prepare space in us to acknowledge our readiness to be filled by the training that follows.

Kendo evolves. Of that there is ample evidence. When I learned kendo at Busen, we were taught the principles of cut kendo and the attitude—always the attitude—of cut kendo. In cut kendo, the student imagines having a real sword that cuts into the flesh. So even when using a *shinai*, this means that the cut remains, even momentarily, at the site of the cut. In touch kendo, on the other hand, the *shinai* bounces off the site of the touch. Today in the United States there are few dojos that are predominantly Japanese. The focus now is on kendo as sport. This is a major concern to many older, traditional kendoists. Some of them say sport kendo is not "real" kendo because it is touch kendo, not cut kendo. To these purists, only cut kendo is the real thing. But what is "real" is what is. Today real kendo is sport kendo.

I am often asked how to teach kendo spirit without cut kendo, how to teach the values of tradition and *Do*—in short, how to focus on the sword as an expression of the self to heal and bring peace, to create life. This is the attitude of cut kendo to create *Do* that I try to help my students create by practice. It is the only wisdom I know, so I tell them, "If it works for you, good. If it doesn't, try something else."

~

A poem composed by Mushanokoji Saneatsu (1885-1976), a writer and artist widely known for paintings of flowers, now hangs on a wall in my daughter Charlotte's home.

Kono Michi Yori
Ware Wo Ikasu Michi Nashi.
Kono Michi Wo Yuku

Other than this path
I have no other path to take.
Thus I take this path.

Michi is simply defined as "the way of." But there is nothing simple about it. In Japanese, *Michi* uses the same kanji as *Do*. The origin of the word *Do* is the Chinese *Tao*, and the kanji depicts footprints on a path. Thus, *Do* can be connected to traveling a "path" or "road" of life with an unfathomable destination. But this requires action or practice. The purpose or objective of kendo can be expressed as *Kendo wa Ken no Riho no shuren ni yoru ningen keisei no michi de aru*. This means that the purpose of kendo is to train diligently by endless repetition with the sword according to the natural law. The goal is to create a decent human being, to free us from the fears and doubts and self-centeredness that diminish our daily lives. To me, this means *Katsu Jin Ken*, or "the sword that creates life."

The development of *Do* has a long tradition and has evolved over time to not only create technical perfection but spiritual realization as well. There have been many attempts at defining the philosophy or elements of *Do*. I believe intellectual knowledge of *Do* is impossible, just as it is impossible to intellectually grasp the beauty of a mountain. Thus, it cannot be put into words.

The Way is not easy or fast. It requires hours and hours of practice. I advise my students to put everything they have into *keiko*. Practice of *katas* is important. The five greatest twentieth-century senseis—Naito Takaharu Sensei, Monra Tadashi Sensei, Negishi Shingoro Sensei, Tsuji Shimpei Sensei, and Takano Sasaburo Sensei—established the *kata*. They felt that it allows practice of more than just sword techniques because it is based on their understandings of Miyamoto Musashi. At Busen, we were permitted to use the techniques of *gekiken* (a form of free fencing practice) as well as *kata* in order to develop training as the *Michi*. Indeed, that was the reason that Naito Sensei left Tokyo and went to Kyoto.

The more advanced stage of sword practice involves practice of *kirikaeshi*, coordinated cuts with movements that are used against an opponent. At Busen, for the freshmen, *kirikaeshi* was practiced six days a week, every week, for a full year. Today, I know of no dojo that practices only *kirikaeshi* for an entire year or even for the entire duration of one lesson.

Musashi discusses the three *Sen* in the "Fire Book": *Ken no Sen* (I attack first), *Tai no Sen* (I wait for my opponent to attack), and *Tai Tai no Sen* (We attack simultaneously). However, all three mean that I attack a micro-fraction of a second ahead of my opponent (the *teki*). This is possible due to the *seme* created in the relationship by *Sen*. So I believe there is only one *Sen* to remember. If I create the relationship, I am in control; I can create any of the three *Sen*. If I am in control, I can win. All three *Sen* are practiced in the *kata*.

Seme is defined in the dictionary as "attack," "offensive," and "assault." It borders on the edge of being disrespectful. The attitude of cut kendo is that of a life-and-death situation. *Seme* is calm, relaxed without a trace of eagerness or tension. Ogawa Kinnosuke Sensei and Ono Soichiro Sensei were untouchable because they sensed their *teki*'s intentions, and their *seme* was so powerful, their pressure so great, that no one could penetrate it.

Another key concept in kendo in addition to *seme* is *zanshin*. *Zanshin* occurs when the sword and the swordsman are one (*itchi*). It is an essential part of *kata* when the prescribed motion has ended; the *shi dachi* pauses ready for the *uchi dashi* to move, always alert.

The kanji for *zan* and *shin* can be read in two ways: *Kokoro wo*

Nokosu, which means, "I consciously induce my spirit to remain." And *Kokoro ga Nokoro*, which means, "My spirit is bottomless, alive with endless, spontaneous energy." The first definition applies to the beginner, the latter to the very experienced. It is the difference between conscious action and unconscious potential. If you have to think about it, it is too late. Even when the battle is supposedly concluded, when the kendoist is exhausted, there is still the unconscious reservoir of spirit. There is an old Japanese saying: *Katte kabuto no o wo shimeyo*, which means "The mind is not distracted by illusion." Nothing is finished; my spirit remains.

Takano Sasaburo Sensei stated, "There is nothing other than *seme*." True spirit cannot be subdivided into parts or seen as a skill to be turned on for *kata* or tournaments and turned off when it is not needed. It is the steadfast, centered spirit, uniting physical presence and emotional attitude with a relaxed potential power.

Ma ai is the relationship or distance between you and your *teki*. It is demonstrated in the *kata*, in which three distances are practiced: long range; close range (within a step of contact); and no range (touching or within finger range). Sport kendo, which is more dynamic, requires quick decisions to choose which *waza* (techniques and footwork) are best to gain the advantage to get a strike and make a point. The further you are from your *teki*, the safer you are. But the *teki* is safer as well. So obviously, the closer you inch into the desired striking distance, the easier it will be to reach the *teki* and make the strike.

The kanji for *ma* means space. Space is vast. One needs only to see Japanese art and calligraphy, as well as the minimal use of furniture, to know that space, or what is not seen, is as important as what is seen. Space is dynamic with creative possibilities. And there is another *ma ai* that goes beyond the visible, whether static or dynamic. I call it "spiritual" *ma ai*. This is the *ma ai* of kendoists like Ono Soichiro Sensei, who serenely fills the space with *seme* and waits in striking position until the opponent approaches to make the strike.

I had this kind of experience in the early 1950s, when I practiced with Ono Sensei. I felt that he was very far away, and I couldn't touch him. When I jumped in anyway, he hardly moved and tapped me on my *men*. Then I felt that his *shinai* point was right in front of my eyes. When I moved to strike, thinking he was close, I still couldn't touch him. This bothered me tremendously. I could not reach him no matter how hard I tried. In short, I was in his *ma ai*. He seemed very far away or very near to me, yet he seemed never to move. I felt like an angry child held at bay by an adult, my frustrated swings thrashing in empty space. This is the goal—to keep the *teki* in close range, enough to make a strike, while at the same time making the *teki* feel at an unreachable distance. Of course, achieving this goal is not quick or easy.

Another word for *seme* is tension. I saw a calligraphy of *Tsuyu Do Do* by Haga Tadotoshi Sensei in Koike Shinichi Sensei's home after *keiko* at the Seattle Kendo Club. It affected me profoundly. *Tsuyu* is a dewdrop, one tiny dewdrop, suspended on a tip of a leaf hanging from a branch, Its shape attracted me, and I stared at it intensely. As I gazed, it seemed to build more and more tension. It felt like I was watching a suspense movie. When will it drop? *Do Do* is like a dam, holding the dewdrop. Finally, the dam breaks. Surface tension builds gradually and naturally as gravity pulls it toward the ground. It's beautiful. But it is also deadly like the water released from the broken dam that destroys everything in its path.

This is the tension between or the relationship between the *uchi tachi* (the senior partner) and *shi dachi* (the student) in *kata*. The *shi dachi* is the dewdrop, the *uchi tachi*, the leaf. The branch is part of the ancient tree, like the dojo, whose roots are nourished by the greater tradition that all the masters of the Way, the *Do*, have traveled. Like the dewdrop, the *shi dachi* has no desire or strain. It keeps on developing in its own natural way. If the leaf moves first, the dewdrop will drop from the tip of the leaf without any hesitation or reservation. If the leaf does not move, the dewdrop will fall naturally, when gravity commands, also without hesitation or reservation. The drama is played out in quiet, seemingly slow motion.

When I think of the dewdrop and the leaf as *shi dachi* and *uchi tachi*, I also think of how the leaf supports the dewdrop, the relationship between the two, until the leaf moves from pressure, perhaps created by the wind or the force of the *shi dachi's hara*. When I think of gravity pulling the movement, I think of the ground, the *hara* centered, which moves naturally. There is no thought involved. And when I think of the release when the dam breaks, I think of the cut, the powerful strike, which is quiet, absolute, emotionless, and without doubt or regret.

This is the perfect balance, the reconciliation of power and calm, that occurs after decades of practice when spirit, sword, and body are one, *Ki Ken Tai Itchi*. The calligraphy of *Tsuyu Do Do* reminds me of Ono Soichiro Sensei's calligraphy, *sei shin* (Quiet Mind), drawn on a small sheet of silk. I had never thought of the concept of *sei shin* until recently when Ono Sensei's wife sent the calligraphy to me after he died at the age of ninety-four. The last thing he did before he died was to take the train from his home in Tokyo to attend a kendo tournament in Kyushu. Ono Sensei's practice developed such a powerful, quiet spirit—a *hara*—that his *seme* was invincible, his timing and strike flawless. Every move he made was as powerful as the water breaking through the dam and as natural and as perfect as the dewdrop falling silently back to the ground. There was wind in Ono Sensei's *ken*.

~

We all make choices in our daily lives and at different stages in our lives to support our physical needs, to find work, to take care of our families. But someday we will have to retire from our occupations. Even sports and hobbies are short lived. I don't know if kendo will become just another sport, a game, nothing else but passing out trophies to winners. Indeed, it is a good sport, an exciting sport. But I hope it will retain the *kata*, remain the Way through *kata*. I think it will because the *Do* is eternal.

Katsu Jin Ken means "the sword that creates life." The sole purpose for me to study kendo is to create life in myself to become a better human being. Military training teaches how to kill. What gives me the right to kill? The dojo allows me to take the path to teach me how to die so that I realize how to live NOW. The sword is always with me, in my spirit, to teach and guide me, to polish me to become better every day and every moment so that I can serve my friends and my community until my usefulness is exhausted. This is my way to try to do *Katsu Jin Ken* for myself and to share *Katsu Jin Ken* with my friends and students. Kendo is my life. It has been the path, the *Michi* to the door to eternal life, the *Do*.

Calligraphy of *Katsu Jin Ken* (drawn by Sensei Aaron Garlick, Taos Kenyukai)

EPILOGUE

Charlotte Kazumi Omoto

My father became ill in mid-April 2013. He had chosen a few years earlier not to have extraordinary measures taken to prolong his life. So in May, after a couple of weeks in the hospital, Dad and I decided that he should return to the assisted living home where he had been living since February. He had made friends with other residents and staff in the short time that he lived there.

As the end approached, he asked to see Yukawa Sensei, the former minister at the Tacoma Buddhist Temple and a good friend. When Yukawa Sensei and his wife, Michiko-san, visited, Dad, along with the sensei, repeated the following Buddhist saying:

われ今幸いに
まことにみ法を聞いて
限りなきいのちをたまわり
如来の大悲にいだかれて
安らかに日日をおくる
謹んで
深きめぐみをよろこび
尊きみ教をいただきまつらん

Ware ima saiwaini
makoto ni minori o kiite

Kagiri naki inochi o tamawari
Nyorai no daihi ni idakarete
Yasuraka ni nichi-nichi o okuru
Tutushinde
Fukaki megumi o yorokobi
Toutoki mioshie o itadaki matsuran

How fortunate am I to be able to hear
The Nembutsu Teachings, now,
Without limit live my life to its fullest in tranquility,
Peacefully living each day by day.
I rejoice in the profound depth of grace of Amida
Receiving the precious teaching of the Nembutsu.

The next evening he passed away.

ACKNOWLEDGMENTS

This whole project began when Diane Kelly Riley introduced me to Norbert Elliot, Acquisitions Editor of Purple Breeze Press. He connected me with one of their editors, Rebecca Mlynarczyk, who suggested wonderful changes that greatly improved the flow and impact of this story about my father. She also found historical records and more contemporary references to my father for which I am grateful. This book would not have happened without her contributions.

I would also like to thank my cousins Sandy Keepers and Swasti Bhattacharyya for information about my father's early life in Hawaii that he shared with their mothers. There are too many of Dad's kendo and Buddhist Temple friends to thank each one personally, but I am forever grateful to them for making his life so rich.

Most of the photos in the book are from my father's collection, but Rebecca found some historical photos, and Aaron Garlick of the Taos, New Mexico, Kendo Club provided the calligraphy of *Katsu Jin Ken*, a key concept in the book.

ABOUT THE AUTHOR

Charlotte Kazumi Omoto is Professor Emerita of Biology at Washington State University in Pullman, Washington. She was born Kazumi Omoto in 1951 in Matsue, Shimane-ken, Japan, and immigrated to the US with her parents and sister when she was ten. She received her BS in biology from the University of Washington in Seattle and her PhD in molecular biology from the University of Wisconsin, Madison. She did post-doctoral work at Princeton, Caltech, and Penn State University, accepting a position in the biology department at Washington State in 1984. She has written professional papers in her field of cell biology and genetics and is the co-author of *Genes and DNA: A Beginner's Guide to Genetics and Its Applications*, a text for non-biology majors. An updated version of this book was published in 2015 under the title *Genetics and Society*. In retirement, she enjoys birding and studying native plants.

www.ingramcontent.com/pod-product-compliance
Lightning Source LLC
LaVergne TN
LVHW091813110826
845146LV00006B/987